I NEVER SAID GOODBYE

Reynold Burrowes

HANSIB

First published in Great Britain by Hansib Publications in 2016

Coinciding with Guyana's
50th Anniversary of Independence

Hansib Publications Limited
P.O. Box 226, Hertford, SG14 3WY

info@hansibpublications.com
www.hansibpublications.com

ISBN 978-1-910553-40-4

A CIP catalogue record for this book
is available from the British Library

Production by Hansib Publications Limited
Printed in Great Britain

To my late wife
Rosanne Callerame Burrowes
and to our son
David

CONTENTS

PREFACE

Attending school abroad in the US, UK or Canada had long been a wistful dream of mine, as it was for my friends, their parents and mine. But implicit in that dream was the expectation of our eventual return home to put our newly acquired knowledge to work for the welfare and betterment of our home country. Alas for my generation things did not work out as we imagined. I have since discovered, however, that there is much truth in Robert Burns' verse about the "best laid plans."

In the blink of an eye 35 plus years went by, and a new family, new friends, and indeed a new "home" country had become my reality. Although in those intervening years I had often thought of Guyana Trinidad and Barbados with affection, life in America was good and fulfilling and I was focused on maintaining it. While I kept in touch with relatives and friends back home and gleaned some local news from them, I had never again given serious thought to resettling there, or even returning for a visit.

Until, that is, I learned of a first-time reunion of my high school classmates and dear friends, all of whom had scattered around the globe, and had become expatriates like myself. I began to picture their faces, the streets we lived on, our youthful hangouts, our teachers, the foods we ate, the nicknames we gave each other. I became uneasy when I felt emotions I had not uncovered or dealt with for decades came flooding over me as I saw the names I had long forgotten who had expressed an interest in attending. Thinking about home brought further anxiety when I realized that I could no longer remember the order in which certain streets ran, or the dates of events that I once recalled automatically. I found myself flooded with emotion and, at long last, a powerful desire to go "home".

I certainly expected to see changes and I planned to document these in a travel journal, but it was the change I never anticipated that most amazed me. In our youthful arrogance, we had fully expected to return to Guyana from schools abroad, hailed by our countrymen as the newest generation of reformers and political players. But there we were after an almost four decades absence, returning to find that we were not even missed, that our country had forged ahead, indeed prospered, without us. We found ourselves, all successful, accomplished men, suspended in an early 70's time warp, quite proud of – yet increasingly disoriented by – the progress we witnessed in the country we once called "home".

It was never my intention to challenge or endorse whether or not we can "go home again". But I have discovered that the home of my youth had changed and the youth I once was had changed also. "Home," it turns out is a fluid concept.

INTRODUCTION

I still vividly remember the article I read as a child, or was it just before Guyana became independent in 1966. The headline read, "Guyanese returns after 50 years". As I did even then, I read the article carefully and, although I cannot recall exactly what it said, the headline has always stayed with me. Why? I don't know. Perhaps it was because all I thought of back then was, "How am I going to get out of this place?" You see, I always knew I would get a university education and become a professional. My father had sat me down on more than one occasion and told me so, my mother had worked to instil that in me and, most of all, I dearly wanted that for myself. What generated much of my anxiety was that I knew I was only a C student and had little hope of accomplishing my dreams. C students did not go to universities. Not from a country that did not have a recognized university of its own, and not when there were so many people grasping for every scholarship foreign governments offered. What made my circumstances especially painful was the knowledge that I had done so well before entering high school at St. Stanislaus. Deep in my soul I knew I was smart but I did not have the discipline and resolve to demonstrate it. Seldom did a day go by when I did not spend some time dwelling on my predicament. Rather than buckle down on my studies, I spent time daydreaming about getting out of school and plotting my path after high school. Many of my friends simply grinned when I would confidently announce my plans after leaving school. I never wore my frustration on my sleeve, but was pained at letting myself down time and again. After all, my father was spending

$25 a semester on a private school, a considerable sacrifice for us, and I was not showing results. That might have been one reason why I read the newspapers so diligently every single day, hoping perhaps that by keeping on top of the news I might find a way to achieve my dreams.

I still recall clearly the many days I spent on the veranda of our house at Supenaam on the Essequibo Coast thinking about going abroad, and cursing the fact that mine was the only family without a relative who had done so. Why was my family so easily complacent I wondered as the sunny days drifted by the lazy Essequibo. Like so many others, I knew Guyana was well behind the advances taking place in developed countries far away. The fact that a big change was on the horizon was evident every time I listened to the BBC news, Voice of America or read the magazines that were passed from hand to hand until they literally fell apart. Despite the fact that our politicians were squabbling like wild dogs over a carcass, my parents and I, and the children in the five prominent high schools were all preparing for change whenever the dust settled. The daughter of my father's cousin Edward was the first of a trickle of graduates who began to return after attending university abroad. We were all proud of her from afar even though she never spoke to any of us, choosing instead to remain aloof, even as her father and his brothers would cross the road against oncoming traffic to greet their country cousins. The backwardness of our country might well have been the reason why the woman in the aforementioned headline had not returned for so many years. Although I often said that would never happen to me now, after all these years, that is precisely what did happen. I had not been back to Guyana for 37 years. Why? I cannot give a satisfactory answer except to say "life" intervened.

Over the years two friends, Horace Nurse and Cynthia Massay Thomas have visited the US intermittently and brought me news from home, but as more time passed their news seemed more remote from my interests. What was curious about my decision to return was the anxiety I began to feel as I contemplated making the trip. Anxious because I knew I had broken a promise to myself made so long ago and anxious because of what I might find. The last time I was home in Guyana was for the year between 1975-1976. I had returned to do some research for my thesis. At that time the once orderly colonial society, then an independent country, was even more in a state of flux than at any time I could remember. Many of my friends had gone abroad to study or had emigrated. Back then I naively thought that this was only a temporary situation and that we would all eventually come back to make our contributions to support our own society. By this time, my father had died and my mother had already decamped to New York where my two brothers were students. Yet I still felt at home in Guyana because my adopted grandmother, Retty Greaves welcomed me warmly upon my arrival. Retty Greaves had been my guardian in Georgetown throughout my high school years and she and her family became part of my extended family while my parents remained on the Essequibo. Living at Granny's helped me forget that my own family was already in the US. I spent my days studying at the national archives and my evenings visiting acquaintances and thinking about what I would do next. On one occasion, I went into a quasi-government office on an errand connected with our house. I was about to depart when I looked up and saw a face I recognized: it was Mr. Carter. He had gone abroad on a scholarship to study at an East European university. "When are you guys coming back home?" he shouted at me standing at the door to his office. Carter was much older than I and, though we knew each other by sight at St. Stanislaus, our high school, we had never spoken. Without showing much surprise, I answered him, "When I am finished. I am not finished yet."

Looking straight at me with penetrating eyes and a slight smile on his face he continued, "People like me feel quite lonely. We are waiting on people like you to come back." Arrogant as I was at that time, I walked out of the office feeling pretty full of myself, and not too sympathetic for my "lonely" friend.

Even though I was still a student in good standing at the Fletcher School of Law and Diplomacy at Tufts University just outside Boston, I knew that my nationality might present some problems getting back into the United States. For at that time the US was, as Guyanese would say, "giving Guyanese a hard time" about leaving or returning to the US. In anticipation, I had alerted people at my school about the situation before I left and was assured they were prepared to send me any documents I might need to return. Armed with these assurances I presented myself to an officer of the US Embassy in Georgetown. Even though my papers were all in perfect order the officer said, "Sorry, we have reason to believe you are returning to the US to stay. You will get married and stay in the U.S.," she said emphatically. How did she know? I thought I had not made up my mind to get married. It was only a possibility then, but she made it sound like a *fait accompli*. I left my interview dejected but asked to see the Ambassador himself. He was a good friend of the Dean at Fletcher, and I was told I could call on him. He invited me to lunch, only to tell me that he could not intercede on my behalf to overturn the decision of a competent officer of his embassy.

I promptly booked a ticket to Montreal from where I believed, as I had heard from the immigrant grapevine, that I could reach the US. Throughout my time in Guyana doing my research, my American girlfriend Rosanne wrote me a letter nearly every other day to keep me informed on what was happening with my friends in Boston.

Returning to the US was the culmination of an interesting journey for me. While little went right for me at St. Stanislaus, everything seemed to fall into place the moment I left high school. For the first time in my life I started working hard and found that I enjoyed it. At every turn I was helped and encouraged and I made the most of every opportunity. Back in the US I married my girlfriend Rosanne but was well aware that, under the terms of my Fulbright Scholarship, I could still be sent home despite my marriage to an American. Having told my employer that I was already a permanent resident by dint of my marriage to an American, I expended a lot of emotional energy in that regard until the Immigration Department finally relented and cleared my status as a permanent resident. I was recruited by three major NYC banks and chose JP Morgan. My wife found a job with IBM in Albany, New York and was transferred to Manhattan within a year. It was a glorious time to be a young couple in the city. After a year living in an apartment on Manhattan's West Side, we bought a two-bedroom co-op in Park Slope, Brooklyn. Living in Brooklyn gave me an opportunity to see my Guyanese friends who had visited here from time to time. It also gave me an opportunity to attend events like the West Indian Day Parade and festivities for national holidays.

When Rosanne was transferred to work at the IBM offices in Westchester, New York it quickly became apparent that we had to move. With that move, however, I was effectively cut off from even the most casual contact with other Guyanese. Like most commuters, I caught the early train into New York City and tried to depart as soon as work ended.

When Rosanne died after 25 years of marriage, however, I got a flood of calls from Guyanese friends I had not seen for decades. They offered to fly in for the funeral and to help me overcome my grief. It was very touching that, after not seeing or hearing from so many friends for so long, they would call to express their sympathy and offer to help. Despite my protestations, they called me often to make sure I was doing well. So, in addition to my in-laws and dear friends I also reconnected with a group of Guyanese from home.

By that time returning to Guyana for a visit had long ceased being a priority for me. But when my friend Pamela Benfield said she was coming to New York to attend a St. Rose's Convent reunion, my interest was rekindled. Pamela had become a friend through my friendship with her brother Ronald Benfield, a high school classmate at St. Stanislaus College. I accompanied Pamela to two events at her reunion and quickly realized how detached I had become from life back home. The most striking was that St. Rose was no longer a girls school, but had gone co-ed so there were a number of men at the reunion. I went up to Alison Friemann and asked immediately for her brother, my friend Bernard, and was surprised to learn he had moved from Montreal to New York City. When I saw Alison again on another occasion she said Bernard had asked her to be sure and get my address and phone number, and to let me know he had been searching for me.

I took the next Friday off to meet Bernard, leaving my home in Riverside, Connecticut two hours early. Despite not having seen each other for over thirty years we recognized each other immediately. We went for a drink at the Warldorf where we spent nearly two and a half hours renewing our friendship. Bernard was no longer the strikingly handsome and athletic young man I last spoke to on the road in front of the Queen Victoria Law Courts in Georgetown. Gone were the chubby cheeks he once had. His slimmer face looked longer because of his receding hairline. The slim grey sideburns and goatee made him look older at first blush, but this impression was quickly erased as he moved his 6'1" frame with vigour as he walked. As he spoke his tight smile and serious demeanour reminded me that he remained the measured and intense individual he had always been. While he did not have a pronounced girth he had become heavy around his midsection, a long way from the ardent and athletic cricketer he once was. The one thing that had not changed, however, was his sharp mind and, even more surprising, his interest and knowledge about affairs in Guyana and the Caribbean. He seemed to know so much more about the politics and economics of Guyana than I did, and was so passionate about it as we spoke that I found myself a bit chagrined. We discovered to our surprise that he lived in Old Greenwich, Connecticut for years while, at that time, I lived a short drive away in Rye, New York. We both took the same line to and from work every day, and yet we never met! Bernard had become the corporate executive he always dreamed of being, an expert in the insurance industry, and yet he had retained the same humility, respect and gracious ways he always showed for everyone he met, especially his friends. The fact that most of his friends are still unaware of the stature he attained as a corporate executive is a testament to this.

I had made an exception to my schedule to meet my friend. I was still suffering from the grief of my wife's passing as was my son David. I had been determined to devote all of my time to seeing my son through this difficult period in his life and so I had put off all social engagements for a while. Some two years later, just as I was beginning to emerge from my social hibernation, an email arrived from Bernard Friemann suggesting we again meet for a drink. I agreed to do so as soon as I returned from a trip to India with my son.

At that meeting my friend looked a little pale and subdued. He said he had been dealing with some serious health issues but was now on the mend. In the interim he had travelled to Canada to join a group of classmates who referred to themselves as "the 59'ers" for a weekend of fun, and he offered to put me in touch with them. The thought of a weekend of drinking did not appeal to me but when Bernard mentioned that John (Carpy) Carpenter had travelled from Guyana, where he continued to live, to Canada for the event, my interest was piqued.

In the meantime my mother fell ill and went into the hospital and I began to think about her family in Trinidad. I called my cousin Janice in Brooklyn and got the telephone number of my Uncle Pusher in Trinidad. After his surprise at hearing my voice for the first time in so long and his dismay at learning about his sister's declining health, we caught up a bit on each other's news. As we were about to conclude our conversation, he said,

"When are you coming home to see us?"

"I don't know. Sometime soon," I assured him.

"I lost your features, man," he shot back.

His simple words sent an arrow deep into me. The thought that if we were to pass each other on the street and not recognize one another disturbed me deeply.

When Uncle Pusher and then his brother, Uncle Carl died in quick succession, I was again jolted by my diminishing connection with my relatives. My frequent excuse to my American friends that I did not return home for a visit "because everyone from the Caribbean visited New York so there was little imperative for me to return," did not apply to these people, and it began to sound hollow even to me as time went on. It was an excuse that was only partly true, for most of my friends who visited New York were professionals and travelled regularly. I thought more and more about my relatives back in the Caribbean, in Trinidad, in Guyana and in Barbados. My thoughts centred on my mother's only remaining brother, Uncle Kelvin. I thought about him because of our past relationship. I fondly remember each of his visits to Guyana. I must have been five or six when he first arrived for a three month visit when we lived in New Amsterdam, the second major city in Guyana. He had travelled by boat from Trinidad with a trunk so large that we children could fit into it. Among the presents he brought for each of us was a leather-bound chess set with a backgammon set on the reverse side.

My brothers and I loved it and we played checkers for hours every day for years. Two years later we were older and living on the desolate Essequibo Coast. We quickly tired of playing checkers and wanted most to learn to play chess. For years we asked everyone who came to our house to teach us to play and no one could. We never even bothered to find out about the other game on the inside of the chess set. It was called backgammon. We just did not know the type of people who could teach us. It was not a question of money; although my father was not rich he would have paid for us to learn.

With those fond memories bubbling in my mind I wrote and invited Uncle Kelvin to come to the US. At the age of eighty-one, he arrived in the US for his first visit. He stayed with my cousin Janice in Brooklyn for the first week and my son David and I went to see him. He did not look like an "old man" as his age might have suggested; instead he stood erect as ever with an untrimmed moustache and an unshaven face. His receding hairline displayed hair that was black and white thus making him look younger than he was. After greeting each other and introducing my son, we posed for pictures with other family members I had never met. I soon found out how fit he was when, with no alcohol in the house, I invited him to go for a drink at a local establishment. When we returned to my cousin's fourth floor walk-up, I huffed and puffed as I ascended the stairs. I watched as Kelvin went in front of me skipping stairs as he ascended and got to the top before me. "I walk everywhere," he proudly said to me as I finally arrived. He spent a week in New York and then flew to California where he spent two months visiting my mother while he stayed with my brother Noel and his family. Back on the East Coast he stayed with me in Riverside, Connecticut for three weeks taking in sights in New York City and the suburbs. His visit was valuable to me and I hoped it was for him also. Not once did he mention any disappointment he may have had with family members who never "sent for him". Rather he relished being from Trinidad and recounted for me the social and economic progress his country had made. His visit brought me one-step closer to making a decision to return home for a visit.

When Bernard Friemann met me for a drink months later, he had a surprise for me. Our classmates in Canada had decided to return to Guyana for their next reunion and wanted as many people as possible to attend.

"Are you thinking of going?" I asked.

"I am thinking about it seriously."

"When were you home last?" I asked.

"I've never gone back," he replied, his face quivering with emotion. "I never got to say goodbye. I never got to say goodbye." Sitting directly opposite to him at a small table in the bar I realized that my friend was close to tears. His face became pale and his voice seemed to tremble ever so slightly. As he reached for his glass to take a sip of wine he added,

"I would like to see my grandfather's grave."

Realizing the moment I interjected quickly, "I never got to say goodbye either. I never thought I would never go back." As I spoke I realized how passionate Bernard felt about having left, despite his enormous success in corporate life in both Canada and the USA. There was obviously something missing. I told him I would think hard about joining the reunion group. That evening as I drove home it began to snow. The snow was heavy, coming down in huge flakes and melting as soon as they landed. It made driving just tricky enough so that I had to moderate my speed. I kept replaying Bernard's near breakdown, his saying, "I never got to say goodbye. I didn't know I was leaving forever." All I could say to myself was, ditto. By the time I crossed the New York border into Connecticut I had made up my mind that I, too, would travel back home if the others were going. Nearly every one of my friends whom I told laughed out aloud and said, "Boy are you in for a shock."

PHASE 1

I hardly slept the night before my departure as my mood had changed from one of nervousness to one of excitement. Frankly, I felt like a man who had abandoned his family in one country, gone to another, reinvented himself, had a new family and then, after more than a generation, stepped back into his old life hoping to make a connection. I was awake at 1:45 am and waited for the 2:00 am clock alarm but by the time it sounded I was already in the bathroom shaving. I must have been moving slower than I thought because my son David was knocking on the bathroom door asking when I would be finished. He had set his alarm to go off at 2:30 am. After that my pace quickened and I was dressed, packed and ready for a 3:00 am departure to JFK Airport for my flight at 7:00 am. It was an ungodly hour to fly, but I did so deliberately to have some time with my relatives in Trinidad.

It was an easy drive from Riverside, Connecticut with very sparse traffic on the I-95 highway. As we drove along one phrase kept ringing in my ear. It came from my Trinidadian cousin Carol Medford who had called me a few days earlier to wish me a "bon voyage". She ended her call with, "Boy are you in for a surprise! Things that you think should be there are no longer there. Boy are you in for a surprise!"

About an hour and half from Piarco Airport in Trinidad the captain announced there had been a black-out in the capital city, Port-of-Spain and throughout much of the island, but he said the airport itself had its own back-up generators so we were not likely to be affected. I thought to myself that such things only happened in Guyana!

We landed and de-planed and I headed to where I thought my cousin would meet me, but he was not there. I walked to a second door and looked around; he was not there either. I then became frantic because I realized I had no address book, nor did I have anyone's telephone numbers with me. I was so certain that after several letters and telephone conversations my relatives would be there. I asked the information booth personnel to make an announcement, which they did. No response! I stood by the booth for a while hoping that, should they be confused about my whereabouts, they too would think to make an announcement. I stood there for about fifteen minutes when the clerk in the booth offered to make a call for me. I explained I had no numbers so he took it upon himself to make another announcement. There was still no response. By then I was beginning to feel very warm and went outside. I tried the departure area first in case my cousin did not know which area was which. I then walked back along the sidewalk towards the arrival gate. The luggage I was carrying around began to feel heavier and the heat was intensifying. As I passed a sidewalk bar serving beer I thought about sitting down to have a cool one. I didn't, but I made a mental note that it might be one option for killing time if I had to stay at the airport for the rest of the day. I reached the arrival door and joined five or six other people standing there with oversized suitcases waiting for their rides. When I found out they were on the same plane as I was I felt a little better. Just as I was beginning to despair a car pulled up to a sudden halt and my cousin Mervyn Peterson and his daughter jumped out. His daughter Kamilah shot out of the driver seat like a rocket and ran to meet me with a warm embrace. She is a young woman in her late twenties, slim and alert. We first met three years earlier when I made arrangements for my uncle Kelvin Peterson, who was then eighty three, to travel to the US to visit me, my mother (his sister) Angela, my two brothers Noel and Arthur and a few friends. She made his travel arrangements and accompanied him to the US. Mervyn stayed near the front door of the car, as though he were guarding it from robbers. From a distance of a few feet he looked like a very old man. I went over to him and gave him a big hug. We had not seen each other in forty-two years. "What do you want to do?" Kamilah asked. I hesitated for a moment and then suggested we go somewhere quiet to get something to eat, or go into Port-of-Spain if that were possible. To my absolute surprise Kamilah lit up when I said Port-of-Spain. "Let's go into Port-of-Spain. The road is clear today because of the blackout and, besides that, today is Good Friday," she said turning half way around in the driver's seat to face me in the back.

In the car, Mervyn and I struggled to make conversation between ourselves. "When was the last time you two saw each other?" Kamilah asked. It was good that Kamilah asked both of us several questions to get us talking and to jog our memories. After more than forty years apart we had no common memories of place or interaction with relatives, and we had developed no friendship as adults. We travelled for about fifteen minutes along a modern highway before Kamilah pointed to an area saying, "This is Valsayn." I remembered the name, perhaps I even visited the area when it was talked about as a new development of its day. I asked Kamilah to give me a quick tour and she was glad to oblige. It was very interesting to see the suburbs, to see the older houses, some with additions made to them, others completely demolished and other more modern and larger buildings in their place. I enjoyed our short tour and we were soon off to Port-of-Spain. Both Kamilah and Mervyn pointed out to me proudly where the road had been widened to three lanes, and the new additions being made to relieve the terrible traffic congestion around the city.

Within forty minutes we had Port-of-Spain in our sights. I was more than excited. I was somewhat prepared for what a skyline of the new Port-of-Spain might look like. A year or so before I saw an episode of House Hunters International showing a couple from Texas relocating to Trinidad and looking for a rental property. Coincidentally Kamilah had also seen the show so we talked about the buildings and their modern interior. Kamilah assured me the buildings I wanted to see were further up in Diego Martin, a suburb further north. As we got into Port-of-Spain, the city seemed a bit drab at first sight. Many of the old buildings were run down and seemed to be looking up at the new glass towers in the distance. The ubiquitous new construction seemed to make the old buildings look worse. Kamilah zoomed up and down the inner city with abandon as I recalled locations: Fredrick St., Henry St., etc. To me, Port-of-Spain looked small, its streets narrow, its stores downtown out of date. After darting in and out of different streets in the downtown shopping area, I asked Kamilah to take me to Belmont where my grandmother's house once was. As we approached that section of the city, I was even more taken aback. It looked even smaller than I remembered and because the galvanized roofs on so many of the homes were rusting it gave the place a more run-down look. When I reached 45 Norfolk Street where my grandmother lived for nearly 60 years, where her eleven children were raised and all of her grandchildren collected as though it were a clubhouse, I could not readily identify the place. When I got out of the car I could make out the core of the original house. Small modifications had been made years ago, which disguised it for a while. It was only after standing there with Mervyn and his daughter that things began to come back to me. Mervyn pointed out Mackie's tailor shop and I pointed to Norville's rum shop, still there, and Mr. Reid's drug store, closed and awaiting its fate. On the opposite side, Mr. Reid's daughter, now a very old woman, still lived in the house he built. Kamilah had a quizzical look as Mervyn and I each pointed out landmarks and added a little story to emphasize our memory of it.

Even though I understood long before I arrived that things would be vastly different and would appear much smaller after being in the US for some time, I could not shake myself free of adolescent feelings and memories no matter how much I tried. All I could say is that these places of my early youth had imprinted themselves so firmly on my mind I could not lose them if I tried. As I walked to and fro in front of my grandmother Georgiana's house bathed in the bright sunlight, my thoughts strayed to her. She was born in 1888 at the very zenith of the British Empire and exactly fifty years after slavery was abolished in the Caribbean. She had eleven children and no real means of support save being a seamstress for the white upper classes. It was a position she got because of her colour as a mulatto and most of all because of her skill as a dressmaker. Many of her clients, however, paid her in dribs and drabs for her work, sometimes renegotiating her fee after she completed the work. She and her children would often see someone photographed in the newspapers in a dress she made, and commented about how good they looked despite the fact that she had not yet been paid for her efforts. Those were the days of white privilege, the days when we thought all whites were rich. That was far from the truth, of course, but we did not know it then and would never have believed it if we were told, for as everyone knew the Brits were always good at "keeping up appearances". Most of them never had the money we thought they did; they were paid modestly by the colonial government, and were themselves handicapped by having to act "white" to maintain their status in colonial society. Those were not considerations for a woman with eleven children to feed. One summer when I went for a visit, she was agitated about political developments in Trinidad, and quite proud that Eric Williams was seeking independence for the island. She noted with pride that British authorities had threatened to arrest all of those who attended his meetings in Woodford Square. She threw her shoulders back and recalled, "I went out there too. Mervyn, Vonrick and many of my grandchildren had said they were going to that meeting. I said to myself, 'Well! if they are going to arrest my grandchildren, then they have to arrest me too'."

By the time independence finally came in 1964, she had heard first-hand about slavery from her parents and grandparents, celebrated Victoria Day as a holiday, witnessed the decline and fall of the mighty British Empire and saw her country become independent. When she died in 1979 at age 91 she must have been a very satisfied woman. She always urged me, "Take your education," as though it were a medicine for getting well.

My cousin Mervyn had gone back and was standing near the car while Kamilah stood by watching me take in the view of the street as it looks today. They were giving me my space to absorb it all. I felt like asking Kamilah to take me to see Grandmother's grave but I held my request. It was obvious to me by then that she had a plan for my visit. When I got back into the car, Mervyn turned to me and said, "Where to now?" to which Kamilah replied, "We're going to see Vonrick. He's in the Savannah playing cricket." It was one of the landmarks I had forgotten to mention I wanted to visit. The trip to get there was more of the same, with sleek new buildings replacing the stately grand old houses. One such house we passed was empty, its paint peeling. It stood there proud, like a once beautiful woman whose beauty had faded and was looking for someone to rekindle the spark within her, and show she was still a beauty. The field around the Savannah was not as lush and verdant as it once was. There were large brownish red patches all around from the large number of people who use it these days.

Kamilah was the first to spot Vonrick off in the distance. We pulled up alongside him before he recognized us. As he stood there holding his cricket gear in his hand, I got out of the car and walked around it to greet him. I would never have recognized him on the street. Vonrick looked old, his bronze skin looked weather-beaten. He was lean and drawn. I went over and hugged him, then did so again. He obviously had not expected to see me, perhaps thinking I would not go into the city and would not make a special trip to see him. We chatted a little, took some photographs, smiled a lot at each other. When I told him he looked frail he said he was five foot eight, 130 pounds and felt great. He said he was seventy years old and felt healthy, which made me perk up. He played cricket, walked a lot because he did not have a car and was OK. After a brief chat and saying our goodbyes we left him standing with his cricket gear as we drove off. We explored a little of the area beyond the Savannah and then headed west for the main road to Carenage. Again my luck held as the roads were abnormally clear and we could go faster than usual. I saw the new mall, the new stadium and new areas in that section of the city. I was impressed with how modern everything was. The houses, the malls and all of the installations I saw were not copies of what we see in the US: it was their version of what they have seen and appreciated from abroad. We went as far as Chaguaramas and then turned around.

On our way back I asked whether we were going to stop for lunch. Kamilah gave me two options, but I had her choose her favourite so she chose a restaurant in the mall opposite the stadium. I got the distinct impression that while I wanted to have something local to eat, Kamilah wanted to show me a modern restaurant, a reflection of her preference and of her country's similarity with foreign establishments. We parked in a huge parking lot and made our way toward the restaurant, past lines waiting to see a movie, and other fast food places. We walked past an inner courtyard, past a stage set for entertainment and into the restaurant. It was not quite a sports bar, but they did have two flat screen TVs, one carrying cricket and the other showing English soccer. The menu was by no means Creole or limited to local dishes and I opted for the poached salmon.

We talked about my impressions of the city and reminisced a bit. When Kamilah left to go to the bathroom Mervyn turned to me and said, "I have very good children. I managed to give them an education and they have all remained close to me." I could see the pride in his face as he spoke. Then to my surprise he said he wished his parents and others had stressed the value of a good education to him when he was growing up. For a moment, I was puzzled and saddened at the same time because all of the people he was referring to certainly stressed having a good education to me. When I thought about it for a while, however, I understood the reasons for the disparity in our views. My father worked for the government and members of our family saw me being prepared for a future even better than my father had. They encouraged me, but they automatically assumed Mervyn would follow his father and uncles as blue collar workers.

During the time we were having lunch Kamilah was back and forth on her phone texting her sister. As we rose to leave she announced we were headed to see Uncle Kelvin and her sister at Mount St. Benedict, the monastery where they were both spending Easter weekend. As we emerged from the restaurant and made our way past many small shops which were by then open, we came upon a Häagen-Dazs ice cream shop. There was a line of about six people waiting to be served, and Mervyn turned to me and said, "Do you want some ice cream for dessert?" "No," I replied emphatically, "I haven't come all the way here to eat Häagen-Dazs." I think the abruptness of my reply dissuaded him from considering having some himself.

As we left Port of Spain Kamilah wanted me to pass by the Dry River, one of the requests I had forgotten I made. As we turned the bend headed there I thought I recognized where I was, but said nothing. "We have come to the Dry River now," she announced and I added, "And there is where Aunt Gloria Medford, my mother's sister, and her family once lived next to the Luspice." "Yes you are so right Boy you've got a good memory ya know," Mervyn said, "I thought I recognized the place." Kamilah had no idea what we were talking about. She knew the names of the people and that was all.

The drive to the base of the mountain on which the monastery sat was speedy and uneventful. I felt good since it was in the direction of the airport anyway. We drove through the village, past the St. Augustine Campus of the University of the West Indies and started up a winding road. As we made our way up, I could see the afternoon clouds beginning to form in the distance. Eventually we made it to the top, exited the car and found Uncle Kelvin chatting away with a group of people also on retreat. They had just finished one of their sessions. Uncle Kelvin's face lit up as I emerged from the car and ran over to greet him. I had written him personally, as I did others, to tell him of my layover in Trinidad. He sent word to tell me he makes the retreat every year at Easter and would greet me in spirit. Dusk began to roll in quickly as we talked and held hands. He insisted I meet Brother Jordan who taught me for one year while at St. Stanislaus. When my mother accompanied Uncle Kelvin on the retreat years earlier, I asked her to look him up, and based on that introduction years ago he had established a friendship with the monk.

We found Brother Jordan in a small office nearby and greeted each other, exchanged a few sentences, and then I departed hurriedly. The skies above had darkened even more and I was a little worried about catching my flight to Guyana. I could see that Kamilah was a little worried also but she said nothing. We descended the long winding road and, as we did, it actually got brighter for a while. I realized that while up at the Abbey we were above a number of drifting clouds that obscured the light at the high elevation. As we reached the village below, we hit a traffic jam. We turned from one street to the next and came upon yet another traffic jam. All of a sudden the village seemed to be a hive of activity; there were cars everywhere, and bottlenecks at every turn. Kamilah expressed her frustration aloud, "I don't know where all of these people have come from," she said, as a short cut she knew proved not to be. I was concerned that if the main road leading to the airport were just as clogged I would really be in deep trouble. We inched our way out of the village and eventually swung left onto the main highway. To my relief it was clear as cars went zipping by. By that time dusk had fallen and Kamilah had her car headlights on. It was 6:15 pm and I had to be at the airport by 6:30 pm. Conversation inside the car had by then turned to silence. There was no use in my asking how far it was to the airport. Kamilah was driving faster than she had done all day, and at every traffic light positioned her car in a lane to make a fast getaway. She was doing 80 mph at times. I looked at the clock on her dashboard as it hit 6:30 then 6:40. It was clearly not dusk anymore and we were driving in the darkness of night. I knew we were close to the airport, but how close I could not ask. Kamilah was concentrating on getting me there and neither her father nor I wished to break her concentration. At 6:45 I could see the glow of the airport in the distance. Two minutes later the car came to a halt. Without saying anything Kamilah jumped out of the car and was around the other side before I could gather my bags and emerge from the back seat. She hugged me and wished me goodbye. Mervyn remained glued to the front seat but I insisted that he get out and give me a hug goodbye. I gathered my bags and headed to the entrance.

At the departure desks, there were five people in line and three clerks. One clerk was doing nothing on one side and the two clerks attending to passengers were "as slow as molasses in winter". There was literally no one at the airport milling around waiting for departures or arrivals, no distractions and yet it took me nearly fifteen minutes to get attended to for my flight. I was told I had to see the clerk who was doing nothing on the other side a few feet away. No one was working with dispatch. No wonder one of the local papers that day had a front-page article criticizing the national airline's "business muddle" as they put it. Every other aspect of the airport procedure was equally as deliberate. When I grumbled about having to remove my belt and shoes to fly from Trinidad's Piarco Airport to Guyana, the customs officer said to me with a shrug, "Paranoid Americans." There were about a dozen people in the waiting room for the plane to Guyana. I recognized a few of them from my flight in. One of them was an American woman who sat next to me. When I asked her what she had done with her time, she said she had spent it at the airport.

At first I thought it was going to be a small number of us flying to Guyana, but as I waited the place began to fill up. It was clear people did not take the arrival rules for local inter island travel as literally as I did. I was just trying to tune out the din of an ever increasing crowd when through my half closed eyes I saw a person I recognized approaching. I sprang up and called out, "Dale Morgan!" He raised his head and a wide smile broke over his face as he arrived at the seat where I stood. He turned to the young man standing next to him and said, "I told you I would recognize him anywhere. He can't change." Our good friend and classmate Bernard Friemann had alerted me that there was a good chance Dale might be travelling on the same plane with me. "How are you?" I inquired. "I am fine. This young man is my son, Colin. He's is travelling with me to enjoy some of the ribbing we'll give each other when we meet.

I want him to get an education. Not the kind you get from books but the one you get from seeing the interaction between people who grew up together and did things together. I want him to see that."

Bernard Friemann (nicknamed Bunny) had told me a year or so ago that Dale and his wife had separated after more than twenty five years of marriage, and I gathered from our conversations that his son might have been affected badly by the whole event, so I understood the sentiments he was expressing.

"How have you been?" I asked.

"I've been good. I'm doing well. Where do you live?"

"I live in Riverside, Connecticut. It's just outside New York."

"And how is Rosanne"?

"Rosanne died, you know."

Dale's expression changed instantly to one of disbelief. "I wasn't expecting that. How long ago did she die?" I filled in a few details for him. I could see the shock he got from hearing such sad news as he repeated, "No no I wasn't expecting that."

"How is Alison?" I asked

"We got divorced. Officially we are still separated but you know how these things are. It has been a long process." I then turned to Colin and said, "Please tell your mother that I remember her fondly and asked for her. Tell her that my wife Rosanne always said that if she had a daughter she would name her after her. Don't forget to let her know I asked for her." Suddenly Colin who had been standing next to his father nonplussed, broke into a wide smile. "Yeah I will let her know you said that. She will be pleased to hear it." I could see he was pleased that one of his father's childhood friends had something so positive to say about his mother. The way he answered me throwing his head back and leaning to one side endeared him to me. At six feet tall Colin, who was in his early twenties and a little overweight, was dressed in a black

T-shirt and jeans. His T-shirt rose up to expose his stomach as he gestured. His complexion was like that of his mother, the colour of honey. He had a head of long bushy hair almost like an afro, and an unkempt beard and moustache.

I had last seen my friend Dale Morgan a week or so after he was a witness at my wedding in Cambridge, Massachusetts some 30 years earlier. I knew he still had a year or so to get his PhD. at MIT back then and left the area immediately afterwards. I heard he had planned to return to the University of the West Indies at Saint Augustine in Trinidad to teach. He still resembled the Dale I knew in my youth, about 6'1" tall with very long legs, broad shoulders and a broad face. His prominent nose and dark eyes made him immediately recognizable. Despite his few added pounds and a stylish goatee, he remained the lean and fit person I knew as a teen. Dale was always a bright fellow, but since he never seemed to be studying diligently, he was usually overlooked until the grades came in, and then his name would appear among the top students. He was a "regular guy" and never comfortable in the exclusive club of the best and the brightest. His background was somewhat unique. His mother's family was Indian and mixed, and his father's family was African and Portuguese; "mixed up" as people in Guyana would say. When I told him that Rosanne had spent some time trying to find him a year or so before she died he seemed shocked. Google had just become a search engine so she delighted in trying to track down friends with whom we had not stayed in touch. Upon learning this, Dale told me he left Trinidad within a few years of returning, went to teach at Stanford, and then went to Texas A&M before returning to MIT where he had been a professor for fifteen years. In other words, he was hiding in plain sight as we searched for him. Interestingly, even Google did not find him we when last did our search in 2003.

"Well! Since you are single and I am single we should be on the lookout for some women in Guyana," said Dale seeking to set a different tone. Colin seemed to enjoy the suggestion, as he smiled once again, probably embarrassed at his father's suggestion. I said something that suggested a complete lack of interest in such matters, but Dale went on. In speaking we established that he and Colin were flying business class so we would be apart on the plane. However his hotel was sending a car to meet him at the airport and we could possibly share it into the city. It was a short forty-five minute flight from Trinidad to Guyana.

The new Cheddi Jagan Airport was modern with a nicely kept façade with flowers, nicely trimmed hedges and a display of the country's Coat of Arms glowing majestically as I walked toward the entrance. Inside, the modest airport seemed roomy and spotlessly clean. The immigration officers on duty all looked very professional in their uniforms and business-like in their demeanour. After moving easily through both Immigration and Customs I emerged into the Guyanese night around 10:10 pm. The night air was cool, and it would not have been out of place to put on the light jacket I had with me, but I resisted. I told myself I was in the tropics. I was home. I did not need it.

The hotel Dale Morgan and his son Colin were booked to stay at did indeed send an SUV for them. Upon inquiry, the chauffeur did not quite commit to getting me beyond the Herdmanston Hotel and that was OK with me. All I wanted was to reach the city because I knew I could get a taxi there. My main concern was that I wanted to travel into the city with Dale to see his reaction to whatever changes we were going to see. I had completely forgotten my warning that travelling from the airport, particularly at night, was dicey because on a few occasions people were stopped and robbed at gunpoint. By the time the car took off, my attitude had changed completely. I seemed to have lost the inhibitions I had before leaving, telling myself, "I am home. What could go wrong?"

The airport and the area around it were once used as the American Air Force Base during and after World War II. The base was one of many obtained in the Destroyers for Bases Agreement of 1940 between the US and Great Britain, in which the US got bases in British territories from Bermuda to Guyana. The original runway was built by the Americans and since then, major additions have been made, but the airport itself has remained in the same place. The first sign that both Dale and I looked for as we left the airport was the airport gate. It was where a watchman sat in charge of admitting those who had identified themselves and the purpose of their visit to the airport. It was a military installation and security was a paramount concern. Back when I was a teenager in Georgetown, boys would sometimes take an impromptu ride to the airport as a sort of "rite of passage", something you did to prove you had the stamina to ride twenty- five miles to the airport gate and back. Dale was the first to spot where the airport gate had once been and, although it was long gone, the entrance to the property was still clearly marked.

Once on the road to Georgetown the first thing that caught us by surprise was when Dale said, "So they have lights on the road!" "No it must be only for this area," I replied. We kept our eyes peeled looking for known landmarks as though we were last there two years ago, rather than forty. We passed houses lit by electricity, many rum shops, and whenever we saw a sign with the name of a village we alerted each other by calling the name out aloud. The street lights went out for about half a mile but just when we thought we were in the old Guyana the lights reappeared. The number of people at roadside rum shops at that hour was curious indeed and the traffic was light but steady. Our driver had remained mum as we bantered in the car, so I asked him to alert me when we came to the point where the road to Linden began. Dale was better at recognizing a couple of places but most of it was new to both of us. Then the lights on the road were out once more. OK I thought, now we get back to driving in the dark like we used to. Within a hundred yards or so they were on again. At that point the driver said, "This road has lights all the way to Georgetown you know," setting us straight with some pride.

Once he had broken his silence our driver began to assume the role of tour guide. He pointed out the taxis passing us going to Linden. He showed us all of the improvements done to make the road into a two lane highway and those currently underway to expand it even further in some places. We passed Diamond Estate and distilleries with its unique smell of rotten eggs, which was always present as a result of the process used to make rum from molasses. The night air had become so cool that our windows were turned up leaving just a two-inch crack so as to prevent the rushing air from hitting us directly. We recognized Houston Estate where our pal Joe Vieira and his family lived. Travelling at night at fifty miles per hour we could only get glimpses of the changes. Our driver announced he was going to take us into Georgetown from the back through the burial ground. It was not the way we knew so I was hesitant for a moment but I relaxed as he pointed out exactly where we were and gave us a running commentary as we proceeded. The burial grounds looked desolate, and with the palm trees that once lined both sides of the road gone, it just looked overgrown. When we emerged onto Sheriff Street we were at first lost, then stunned. It had turned into a thoroughfare for rum shops, night clubs and restaurants. Dale, who lived three houses in from Sheriff Street did not recognize when we passed! We saw so many massive structures that we both had trouble digesting the changes. We arrived quickly in Queenstown and when we pulled up at the Herdmanston Hotel we found ourselves in surroundings that were much more familiar. After such a sudden introduction on the road from the airport and through part of Sheriff Street, it was good to see some place we recognized. The whole trip thus far had been like going into freezing water after a sauna. My only problem then was that I still had to get to my hotel.

The driver of the SUV decided he would take me to my hotel up the East Coast Highway about six miles away and I was glad I did not have to get another taxi at that hour. I introduced myself to the driver and we proceeded along Peter Rose Street, turned right and then left onto Irving Street. We had just travelled a few blocks when I said out loud, "Oh that's where John Carpenter lives." "Oh you know John Carpenter?" the driver said, "I do a lot of work for him. Johnny is a nice man." I was a bit taken back that a taxi driver would know a prominent business man. It was not the norm and I had heard from Bernard Friemann that John Carpenter had indeed become very well known and successful.

Once we hit the East Coast Road a mass of people appeared in front of me all partying along the sea wall. It was the numbers that stunned me because it was near 11:00 pm. Darwin Grant's reply to my surprise was, "You ain't seen nothing yet." He explained that the crowd was light because it was Good Friday, and that Saturday and Sunday it would be much bigger. As we drove by I could see there were people cooking for themselves and others purchasing from tents set up for selling soft drinks and food. The throngs of people along the sea wall continued for quite a distance. I began to feel tired and longed to get to my hotel. Once again cars were zipping up and down the two lane East Coast Highway. When we pulled into the Grand Coastal Hotel it was just after 11:00 pm and I was ready for bed.

BACK HOME

The one thing I did before flopping into bed was to pull the curtains all the way back so as to allow the light at the break of dawn to come streaming into my room. I was too tired then to even realize which way the window faced. I slept well but somewhere around 4:00 am I was awakened by the steady shrill of the wheels of trucks travelling at high speeds. When I opened my eyes it was still dark outside and for a while I lay in my bed just listening to the sounds of trucks as they passed along with the jitneys. I continued to doze on and off several times before I was startled by my 7:00 am wake up call. By then the morning sun was streaming into my room and I realized the window faced east. I still felt tired and stayed in bed a while longer, but eventually I decided to get a better look at my surroundings. My room was "deluxe" according to the hotel. It had a flat screen TV with cable, telephone, crown moulding a desk and chair. It was very spacious and I wondered if hotel design schools have determined the optimum size of a room required by different categories of travellers.

I had stumbled into the bathroom earlier when the passing trucks first woke me up but I could not get the toilet to flush, so that was the first thing I tried to do once I was up and about. It did not work despite three or four efforts. I picked up the cover to see what the problem might be and in place of the chain which raised the mechanism to flush the toilet, hotel personnel had installed a piece of stiff wire. The wire, not having flexibility, must have gotten stuck in the wrong position but I was able to fix it. Anyone who has as many bathrooms as we do in the US knows how often those chains give out. The bathroom itself was of a good standard size. It had a granite counter, hot and cold running water, and a tub with a shower. I was amused because all during my many years in Guyana I had never seen a tub in anyone's house or even in a hotel, and I certainly never saw hot and cold running water.

The Grand Coastal Hotel was built in the fashion of a motel. Much of the architecture was positioned to take advantage of the strong breeze coming off the Atlantic Ocean which was visible from the verandas and balconies of the upper level. The liberal use of wood in all the public spaces, the office, the restaurant and bar were all designed to give it a local feel. After looking around the hotel I inquired at the office and found out my friend Bernard Friemann had arrived. He was already in touch with Dale Morgan so we agreed to go over to the Herdmandson Hotel for breakfast.

Bernard came downstairs in a nice soft blue coloured shirt and slacks. I could tell he was happy. He said he had arrived the day before and had gone into the city to look around. I did not ask him to elaborate and was glad he didn't because I wanted to see it with fresh eyes. We got a taxi and took off to meet Dale. We travelled along the East Coast Highway surprised at the changes the country had made in such a short time, changes which I thought would have taken far longer than they obviously did. We were travelling on a modern road and there was traffic going both ways, lots of cars and jitneys. Bernard told me the government had gotten out of the transportation business and had given over the whole operation to private enterprises. He said that both taxis and jitneys (which carried 10 to 12 people in addition to a driver and conductor) were assigned numbers to serve specific villages or suburbs.

It was not long before we arrived at the Herdmanston. Once I saw it in the light of day I realized it was the place my friend Cynthia had recommended to me on several occasions. The hotel was comprised of two large bungalows. The one in front housed the office and rooms upstairs; the one in the back, about twenty-five feet away, housed the restaurant and additional rooms. All around the property there were a number of well-tended tropical flowers and plants which gave the place a stately feel.

Once Dale came downstairs we made our way over to the dining room. We took our seats and did a round of what we each had done since we were last together at school. Each person delivered a good piece of his life in quick succession. I then said to Dale, "I did not want to ask you last night when we met because your son was present but what went wrong between you and your wife. I remember her as such a nice person." Dale said he was glad I did not raise the subject in front of his son. He said his divorce was partly what making the trip with his son was all about. It was supposed to be a catharsis for them both. He spoke about the deterioration of his marriage, the acrimonious and prolonged divorce which had been going on for nearly a decade and the effect the whole process was having on his son. As he spoke, especially about the latter, he grew sad and seemed to be doing his best to fight back tears, which might have flowed had he not been interrupted by Bunny who launched into an account of his own divorce and its effect on his children. Bunny, ever the analytical thinker, detailed how he thought the divorce affected his wife and each of his children. As Dale spoke I was sorry I raised the subject but, by the time Bunny was finished, I was glad I did because they both were so eager to share their feelings with someone who would understand. I thought of my wife, of how lucky I was, but I could not help but be a little sad for my friends.

Dale had told us when we arrived that his son Colin would probably not join us for breakfast because he was still asleep when Dale left the room, but we were nearly finished our "salt fish and bakes" breakfast when Colin arrived. "Hi Colin," Dale shouted as he stood in the doorway surveying the dining room. Colin raised his hands in response. Immediately upon seeing him I felt it was clear what he had been doing in his room after his father departed. His overgrown beard was trimmed and neatly shaped, his long black hair was styled and not as wild and knotted. This made his bright eyes look more pronounced. I could see in daylight that he was more like his mother in complexion. His new presentation made him look more like the budding poet his father had told us several times he wanted to become. After greeting us, Colin made straight for the buffet table and gathered a few items before joining us. Dale seemed to be hungrier and wanted some local vegetables, cassava, sweet potatoes, and a few others. He urged Bunny and me to try them and, hesitantly, both of us did. From our first encounter at Piarco Airport, Dale was excited when talking about the food. He seemed to want it all in one sitting even though he did not eat everything he ordered. He called the waitress over and asked, "What else do you have for breakfast?" "We have some hot cross buns that just came out of the oven." "Bring us some hot cross buns," Dale replied. "We simply must have some cross buns!" After deciding on the number, he went into his childhood memory of the preparation, the baking and the smells in the house when his family made them for Easter. As he spoke it was obvious he was trying to engage Colin to see and enjoy his enthusiasm for these memories. The cross buns when they arrived were warm and good. Bunny and I shared one while Dale carved into one by himself. He urged Colin to try it even though he complained he was full. Colin, like his father, was smart and like his father he did not wear his intelligence on his sleeve. He had travelled with about 200 poems for our classmate Mark McWatt, an award winning poet, to look at. By the time we left the table I realized Colin was no slouch, and he was giving his passion a real go. He was his father's son.

While we were sitting at the table enjoying our Guyanese breakfast, Bunny Friemann was constantly on the telephone with a contact who was coming all the way from Vreed-en-Hoop to chauffeur us around the city. Before leaving New York Bunny had made an agreement brokered by his friend Lincoln Van Sluytman to provide him with whatever money he needed while in Guyana, which he would then repay in US dollars upon his return. Immigrants do this sort of transaction all the time but I had never associated it with Bunny, probably because he was an accomplished professional, an accountant no less. That he entered into this homespun agreement surprised me. Why, I wondered, would he be engaged in such a pedestrian manoeuvre.

Bunny attended McGill University then went into the insurance business. He rose to become the President of the Financial Risk Management Division of Reliance Nationals. He was Chief Executive Officer of Minet Risk Services in the USA when it was sold to Aon, thus making him an even bigger player in North America. His modesty and need to maintain a close relationship with his classmates from the old country does not allow him to share his accomplishments with them.

Feeling a bit heavy by then, we left the dining room and walked over to the main building where Dale and his son had their room. They both wanted to retrieve something before leaving so Bernard and I stayed in the air-conditioned office rather than go into the car. A workman came down the steps and said to the clerk at the desk with whom we were having a casual conversation, "The hot water is not on." Her face stiffened with concern. Before she could respond, Bunny interjected in his own deadpan style, "In our day the water heated up when the sun came up. I remember the first time I saw two pipes for different water temperatures in Canada, I was baffled." There was polite laughter. The people to whom he addressed the remark were Guyanese like he was but they were too young to remember not having hot and cold running water.

We went outside and had to decide how four beefy guys were going to fit into a compact car along with the driver. It was not easy but we did. We had no specific destination request, we simply told the driver we wanted to see Georgetown. At first our driver, Sabitree Mohan, seemed a little confused, but she quickly gathered herself as we kept talking and she got a feel for what we wanted to do. We drove along Lamaha Street and turned up Main Street. While driving Sabitree was acting as a tour guide, pointing out where certain places were; she was a natural at it. None of us in the car could comprehend how drastic a change the city had made. Its complete character had been altered. It was like seeing a friend you knew at four hundred pounds standing before you five years later at 145 pounds. As we drove down Main Street, we passed the new church still being constructed on the ashes of the old. We came to the Cenotaph and the old Carnegie Library next to it. By then we were all glad to see something we truly recognized. Even though we all knew the name "Tower Hotel" it looked nothing like the one we remembered except for the name and the real estate it still inhabited. We continued down Avenue of the Republic past Bunny's old work place at Fitzpatrick and Graham, past a shabby looking City Hall. Both City Hall and the Victoria Law Courts next to it looked in desperate need of repair. This, coupled with the ever present garbage on the sidewalks and the overgrown clogged gutters gave us a numb feeling. What happened to the garden city of old? We turned onto Brickdam and went past our alma mater, St. Stanislaus College, which from the outside looked good in comparison to the other structures we recognized. We travelled down Brickdam to Camp Street. The Brickdam Police Station was at least painted and its surroundings somewhat manicured. It was a pleasure to see Catholic Brickdam Cathedral standing majestically, looking clean and well tended. We were still trying to get our bearings, to come to terms with the immense quantity of garbage in the streets and how ragged everything looked when we turned onto Camp Street. It was the route I took four times a day for all of my days in high school so I knew it well; yet I was lost. I kept saying to my friends, "It all looks so small." Bunny offered an explanation. The place looks smaller because they took away the grass parapets to put in parking or add a pedestrian walkway so that sense of space is gone. We had come by then to realize that many of the old buildings taken down were one and two stories high, only to be replaced with much larger structures three and four stories high. Because nearly every new building was built out of concrete, rather than the wood used in our day, the character of the city had irrevocably changed. We had gone from a city of orderly white British-style bungalows to a concrete high rise style of construction. The other notable thing was the number of people and small businesses around. Every doorway seemed to have a little shop, and every corner seemed to have a person or two selling something. It made me wonder where the money to support all of these small businesses came from?

We went up and down several main streets before Dale suggested we go to see where Bunny's old house was. The transformation of Bunny's former residence was a testament to our beloved city now gone. Bunny once lived in a magnificent dwelling on Middle Street. The house was two stories high and stood on stilts some twelve feet high. In a meticulously tended yard there were flowers in the front between the fence and the house. There were five or six fruit trees in the rear and on both sides of the house. Its appearance was that of an estate manager's house on a deep lot. Its setting gave it a majestic feel even though it was in the centre of the city. All of us who went to visit Bunny admired the sumptuous surroundings. When we turned the corner and pulled up in front of the house neither Dale nor I recognized the place. The ground level was enclosed and the front had been extended into the yard. The addition was not flattering to the building but was practical for the office building it had become. We all had blank faces as we emerged from the car. The grass between what was the front fence and the road was paved over to make way for parking. Dale had to urge Bernard to stand in front of the building and take some pictures. Bunny, who had seen his old home the day before we arrived, was reluctant to get out of the car but did so after being prodded. For the people who now owned the building it had long morphed into something else, so they did not share our sentiments and rightly so. Times had changed and they had changed with them. All over the world in every major city similar changes have occurred and are ongoing. While some people grumble to themselves others march in opposition.

Sabitree drove us up and down several streets many times. Someone in the car thought we should break for lunch even though we had had a hearty breakfast, but our excitement in seeing the new city made us use up a lot of emotional energy. I estimated that at least 30% of the buildings had been replaced in the centre of the city by concrete structures. Sabitree agreed to take us to a great local eatery but cautioned that it was a bit out of town. We rode up the East Bank Road leading to the airport and stopped at the M&M Restaurant in the vicinity of the Demerara River Bridge. The place had the appearance of a roadside shack. She assured us the food was good and urged us to forget the appearance. There were two or three lines of a few people each waiting to order. The menu was written on the wall overhead and while we studied the menu several people pushed past us. The front of the building extended so far onto the sidewalk that walking while cars zipped by was dangerous. People parked anywhere and walked past the garbage and dust to get inside. I grabbed a table for our party and told the others to order. Sabitree ran over to me asking, "Chicken, duck or beef curry?" I thought for a minute and ordered chicken.

Sabitree's recommendation was spot on. The ragged look from the outside belied their cooking. Along with our curry chicken we had roti and dalpouri. During our meal, while we were mulling over everything we had seen so far, Sabitree told us that building in concrete had become the preferred way in construction. As a practical matter it was easier to maintain and people wanted to have larger houses to accommodate all of the modern conveniences their parents never had. She told us the roadside restaurant we were eating in started on that spot, and had branched out to three or four other locations around the city. They had also turned themselves into caterers, and were well known for doing parties, weddings and other events. After a leisurely lunch, I strayed into the back to get a glimpse of their operation. Behind the restaurant, they had erected a cavernous warehouse. Some stairs led to an office on a small second level which had a few computers and four or five employees. On the floor level at the front of the building there were women working in groups. They all had on aprons and hairnets and sat in a row peeling different vegetables. Their surroundings were presentable but not clean. The women manning the pots were similarly clad and were sweating from the heat. There was a small enclosure for producing cane juice. One large machine lay broken, while the other which was obviously the one in use lay silent with a dried stem of cane sandwiched between its jaws. Discarded cane stalks lay on the floor. My North American sensibility caused me to wish the sanitary inspectors would pay them a visit! In the rear were burlap bags and pallets of different items used in preparing the various foods they sold. I had to wait my turn to get into the bathroom which was also in this area. Its upkeep was clearly not a priority for the owners. As I walked out of it, I found myself saying, "Well at least it worked!"

Sabitree's next suggestion was totally unexpected. "How about us going over to Vreed-en-hoop and take a look around?

We are here and it's just over the bridge," she suggested. We just looked at each other in total surprise and agreed. We piled into the car and were off. It was our first time going over the bridge, and both Dale and Bunny were particularly animated about travelling over the pontoon bridge, the first bridge over water in the country. We all recalled the politics surrounding the government's decision to build it, the government at that time headed by Forbes Burnham.

I had passed through Vreed-en-Hoop quite often in the past, and was eager to see what had become of the place once the Ferry terminal was closed. Vreed-en-Hoop was once the only way into Georgetown from the Essequibo, the West Coast of Demerara and other parts of the interior. The Stelling, or wharf, was comprised of a massive warehouse and had the only passenger ferry able to bring people into the city of Georgetown. Passengers arrived by trains link from Parika, by car and bicycles. Needless to say it was always packed, so that when live cows were among the items to be transported it was sometimes awkward to get them aboard. Because of its prominent position as a transportation hub, one would often walk past tons of produce stored in the open warehouse ready for shipment to Georgetown on the other side of the Demerara River a mile away. The whole transportation system was then run by the Transportation and Harbour Department. The captain of the ferry and the sailors were always decked out in proper naval attire, white sailor shirts, sea caps and navy bellbottom trousers. It was all pretty impressive and woe to the sailor who did not appear in proper dress to perform his duties. To turn up in their off-duty blue denims, worn for cleaning the boat and other chores, often resulted in a visit from a senior officer from the bridge and a "chewing-out", sometimes in public.

As in the city of Georgetown, there were cars everywhere around Vreed-en-Hoop. Because it was Saturday, a shopping day for many people, the market was going strong. Small stands, large stands and temporary stands were all around selling fruit, vegetables and clothes. The number of people milling around made me wonder where so many people were coming from. There was an obvious energy about the place and I wondered if it was because the country had such a young population. As we drove by, the stands had spilled out of the market proper and onto the streets in the vicinity. I noticed that some stands had imported fruits and vegetables for sale, items that were on sale only at Christmas time when I was a child; fruits like cabbage, grapes, plums and apples. Some of the larger and more permanent stands had a TV going in the background.

After taking us through part of the market, Sabitree wanted to show us the more residential parts of the town. It was interesting to see how much the once sleepy village, formerly dependent on such a slow transportation system, had grown. The streets were all paved and well maintained and the much larger houses here were also being built out of concrete. The trenches around for drainage were not clogged and, unlike in Georgetown, there was very little garbage on the streets. Suddenly we pulled into a driveway and Sabitree declared, "This is my home. I live here with my mother and my aunt. Come in."

I was again surprised at the invitation, but we were all game. Hers was a simple middle class home, painted and obviously well maintained. The bottom house was not fully enclosed and had a port for her car and a small enclosed room in the rear. At the other side of the garage she had erected an altar on a dais about eighteen inches high. The shrine was dominated by a large picture of a Hindu holy man with long hair dressed in a saffron flowing robe. She belonged to a group that follows the teachings of this holy man and had made two pilgrimages to India to the site of his sect. It was clear to us even before we visited her home that she was a devoutly religious person just from our conversation while driving. It was with some effort that her mother was able to come down the stairs to meet us. She had had a heart attack a few years before while visiting her other daughter in the US and, though she had recovered, the episode left her in frail condition. We were introduced also to a cousin who emerged from the room in the rear. She apparently was at the house recuperating from the recent death of her son and was also in a fragile state. As the last child and daughter, Sabitree explained that it fell to her to take care of her ailing mother and repay her for all she had done for her and the older ones who had left home. Her devotion to her religion seemed to give her the comfort to see her choice through. After chatting for a while we departed.

We were much more relaxed in visiting Vreed-en-Hoop, mainly because it was a much more familiar sight. We turned on the main road to explore the part of the street market and especially to see the old stelling. The area was abuzz with shoppers loading up on fresh produce for the week. The Stelling was in a state of disrepair. Towards the entrance of the massive structure there were a few stands selling produce but most of the area lay abandoned, though in good shape for a place not officially in use for more than two decades. At the side of the stelling I came upon a number of small boats which seemed designed to transport passengers, so I inquired. One captain took great pride in explaining to me that they all ferried people who did not have cars to the other side of the river for a small fee. He explained that some people still parked their cars at Vreed-en-Hoop and took the boats because they did not want to drive in the city for "all sorts of reasons". From the number of boats bobbing gently in the water as we spoke, I concluded it must be a good business. But it was interesting to see how a place abandoned by the government had been taken over for use by merchants and shop keepers who rushed in to fill the void. Vreed-en-Hoop had inadvertently restored our sense of balance. The whole town, though a lot more populated and congested, retained the wide parapets and green spaces we were accustomed to and were desperately looking for.

We left the west bank and drove quickly back to the city. Sabitree drove through Charleston and then came to a stop. She turned to Bunny and said, "Vanny asked me to bring you here. He said I should not tell you where you are. I should allow you to guess." "Vanny" was Lincoln Van Sluytman their mutual friend who had put them in touch for their "US dollars-for-Guyanese-services-exchange-agreement". Bunny Friemann was baffled. His face was blank, his eyes opened wide as we stared at him wondering if he would come up with the right answer. Sabitree broke the suspense by saying, "There was a big house here." Bunny was still lost. Then she said, "This is where Vanny's old house was." A smile broke over his lips. The whole area was so transformed by large buildings and concrete he could not comprehend it. "This is where I spent so much time visiting my friends," Bunny recalled. He just stood looking at his surroundings for a while trying to comprehend why he was so stumped.

It was unbelievable how obvious the garbage and clogged trenches were in Georgetown. We went down Durban Street with its overgrown trenches and made it to Sheriff Street to see Dale Morgan's old house. We had been past Sheriff Street before but missed it in the dark. Of all the streets in the new city none exemplifies the changes like Sheriff Street. It was once a minor artery that technically linked the old city to new suburbs like Subryanville. It was dotted with two or three corner stores but the houses that lined the street especially at both ends were predominantly bungalows. It began at the East Coast Highway and dead-ended at the Botanical Gardens. As a result it came alive most often at rush hour. With large ten foot wide trenches on both sides it was not a particularly pretty street but it was functional. In the early 1970's the government extended the street through the Botanical Gardens while simultaneously widening the other connecting artery which ran through Le Repentir Cemetery to the Ruimveldt housing scheme. This development linked two areas with growing populations from new housing developments that needed an outlet. The gates to the sections that passed through the Gardens opened and closed at the beginning and end of each day, thus preserving a limited use of the new link. The decision by the Transportation and Harbour Department to scrap all its train services, a policy advocated by US advisors, increased the need for other types of vehicular transport. Their own attempts to do so failed as their buses could not keep up with the volume of traffic. After private jitneys and taxis took up the slack, the gates through the Botanical Gardens were opened permanently. It did not take the taxis long to realize they could use this new link to bypass the city to get to the airport and make other connections within the city itself.

Once Sheriff Street became a main artery of the city, development followed. Today it is a street dominated by large restaurants, rum shops, appliance stores and night clubs which when they come alive at night are a blaze of sometimes gaudy lights and people jostling to avoid the speeding traffic. These new businesses are housed in these recently erected three four and five story buildings which came as a shock to a returning visitor like myself. As I walked along the street during my visit the steel frame for a six story edifice was being erected. In going vertical Sheriff Street seems to be leading the way. The few bungalows that remain sit fading in the Caribbean sun looking upward as though waiting their inevitable end.

We turned onto his street and Dale found his house immediately. It had changed a bit but not by much. He took some pictures and had his son Colin take pictures of him in front of it. He asked us to take pictures of him and Colin in front of the house. All of the commotion brought the current occupants to the window. Dale explained he once lived in the house and began to reminisce about many of his childhood exploits in the area, pointing out who lived where. I recalled we both went to shoot birds with his air gun in some abandoned rice fields up the road in what is now the suburb of Lamaha Gardens. As he spoke Dale seemed to remember more and more. Then he told us a story.

There was a boy who lived up the road whose father bought him a brand new bicycle. At that time bicycles were the main mode of transportation in and around the city. The first day he rode it proudly and shined it down with a yellow cheese cloth. Dale along with the other boys wanted to have some fun so they took the bicycle and hid it. When the boy told his father he had lost his bicycle his father gave him a spanking and told him to find it. His father spanked him for five successive days for losing his bicycle. At the end of the fifth day when the boys thought he had enough they returned the bicycle. Upon telling his father he had found his bicycle his father spanked him once more for being careless. The boys all thought that was amusing. Dale also recalled that one of his friends lived at the corner so he and Colin walked over to the place. To his surprise, the family still lived there and still operated the business that was there years ago. Dale and Colin went upstairs to meet his old friend and when he returned he said they were able to reconnect with each other. His friend had inherited his father's business and had never left the old neighbourhood. Next, Dale wanted to go to the Kitty area of the city to see where he was born on David Street. Once again we found the house and walked around a bit. I myself had visited David Street quite often in my youth. The woman who washed our clothes lived there so I went every Saturday to take the soiled laundry and collect the clean clothes for the coming week. I also used to travel to David Street to attend mass at the Catholic church. I remember going there on one occasion after I learned that a girl I wanted to see attended that church. Neither Dale, nor Bunny, nor I could remember if the church on David Street was the same as it was years ago. There was a difference but we were unable to figure out what that difference was. The trench in front of the church was fitted with concrete sides, something new that made it narrow and more controlled. Like the others around the city, it was clogged with debris even though the water was running and fish still swam in it. Dale seemed satisfied as we departed but I asked that we drive around Kitty for a little while. We went down William Street where good friends, the Lords, once lived. We did a quick drive-by and then headed back towards the centre of town.

We retraced our steps through Regent Street and Camp Street and ended up at Bourda Market to get some coconut water. Sabitree took us to a man she knew, a stout man of Indian decent. His skin was weathered from standing in the sun all day. His shirt and tattered straw hat were stained from sweat and coconut juice but, despite his appearance, he was business-like in dealing with patrons. He said he had coconut from Mahica and the Pomeroon. I knew about wine coming from different regions but not coconut water. I pointed to one I thought looked good and his hand reached over and tore it off the bunch in one action. He whipped out a cutlass, modified solely for the purpose of his business. It was an ingenious modification and he wielded the instrument with precision and self-confidence. Dale was praising the coconut water so effusively as he drank that I thought for a moment that he could be describing a vintage glass of wine. I realized, however, that he was just wallowing in the sights, sounds and familiarity of being at home with his son. A group of well-dressed patrons arrived at the Indian man's cart and, from the way they spoke and moved, they seemed to have been there before. Again the vendor charged into action without so much as a smile.

The area around Bourda Market looked bleak. The stands from which people sold their wares and produce were old and there seemed to be no particular order to the place. It was as though things developed on an impromptu basis and those in charge just allowed nature to take its course. What used to be called "Bourda Green", an open air patch of green where political meetings were once held, was completely devoid of grass and taken over by a mass of stands. With no authority to restrain them Merriman's Mall has all but succumbed to the same fate. Merriman's Mall used to be part of the water supply for the city. It was abandoned and stood half empty for years until it was filled in and turned into a huge marketplace. Neither the City Council nor any citizens groups ever came up with a decent proposal for the place. Failure by officials to do something constructive with it led to the construction of a group of ragged stands which now blights the whole area.

We took Thomas Street into Albertown and my friends dropped me off at 10 First Street to visit my aunt. Just as I was about to step out of the car Bunny turned around from his front seat and said to us, "What was the one thing we did not see on the roads today?" He waited a few seconds then answered, "Bicycles." We gave each other a blank look. "Bicycles!"

I had written my father's sister, Aunt Olga, two months earlier to tell her of my impending visit and said I would call her on that day around 4:00 pm. Her house had remained the same but there were drastic changes all around. My cousin Yvette Collins greeted me at the door. She and her brother Robert have lived with Auntie for some time. Yvette called upstairs to tell her I had arrived, and within a few minutes she came eagerly down the stairs. As my aunt descended Yvette turned to me and said, "She has a little trouble with her left leg." I could see the smile on her face as I rose from my seat to greet her. "How are you Auntie Olga?" "Boy I never thought I would ever see you again. How are you?" my aunt exclaimed.

We hugged each other. We held hands, looked each other up and down and hugged again. It had been over forty years since I last saw her. I had kept in touch with several family members simply by sending them a Christmas card annually with just a little note scribbled inside. Even though most of them had never replied I continued to do so. Lo and behold about seven years ago Aunt Olga began to send me a card also. Two years earlier when she celebrated her ninetieth birthday I sent her a special card as did my other cousins in the US. Even though Aunt Olga was near ninety three years of age she looked remarkably good. Her hair was black and white and her once plump size had shrunk to the average weight of someone of her 5'6" height. Her sight and hearing were good and she remained alert in mind. We talked about different family members, about my cousin Cyril in New Amsterdam, about Uncle Jack's children and Uncle Harold's children. She was able to tell me something about each of them, how often they visit, when last she saw them, what ailments they suffered from. She got Yvette to give me the telephone number of everyone I asked for. When I told her I wanted to know about my grandmother Margaret McRae's family she smiled. I had never met many of them but kept crossing paths with them. She reminded me that Grandmother had died in 1977 at the age of 93 and had six brothers and sisters. After some time she was able to recall them all. I had never met nor heard the names of her sisters, and to hear the names of two of her brothers for the first time was a bit of news. I surprised her when I told her that I went to Barbados to look for her sister Constance Seargent, who her father left there when he emigrated to Guyana. By then Constance had died but I met her daughter and two sons. She smiled as I broke the news to her even though it was an event that took place so long ago. She told me that as children they had corresponded with her but had just lost touch. After a while the conversation strayed to the condition of her house.

She was particularly upset by the flooding of her house after the unusually heavy rains in the flood of 2005. She told me her house had two feet of water in it and, as a result, the floors had to be completely replaced. At the time of that flood she had lived in her house for fifty years, and in Georgetown twenty five years before that, and had never seen so much water. Even when she lived in Buxton as a child she said there was never that type of flooding. She blamed it on what was going on "outside". Then she elaborated, "They don't clean the gutters along the roadside anymore. Look outside. They are all clogged up with silt and garbage. Everybody knows Guyana is below sea level, we all learned that in school. They drilled that into us, so we always had to keep the gutters and trenches clean."

When I pointed out that it was an unusual rainfall, a one hundred year flood, she said that was one factor only. She said if I were correct, why were there floods two times since then when no rain was involved, just high tides. I was surprised Auntie Olga was so up on local politics, but the large flat screen TV sitting prominently in the middle of her living room told me how she got her news. The flooding of Georgetown in the rains of 2005 was the first event that grabbed my attention for many a year. Seeing the city totally submerged on national TV was surprising, for such a thing had never happened when I was there. The fallout from that event was that nearly everyone had an opinion about what and who was partly to blame. It was sort of like a Katrina-in-New Orleans moment for the government of Guyana as they were blamed either for contributing to the event or not being able to respond to it. My own involvement was personal as my cousin Frank Collins solicited contributions to assist Aunt Olga in restoring her property. Two subsequent episodes, the sea wall breach of February 2012 and the Kingston Koker episode of March 2013 having to do with high tides rather than rainfall, would seem to squash the main argument advanced by the government.

Because 90% of the people of Guyana live on a narrow coastal plane which occupies 7.5% of the country land area, everyone is well aware of their unique problem.

I left Aunt Olga after promising her I would return to visit at least twice more before I departed. I walked down First Street, turned onto Albert Street and walked down the length of it towards Croal Street. By then the fog I was in, being a place I knew and felt at home in but could not recognize, had lifted just a bit. It was a lot to process in a few hours. By that time on Saturday the afternoon crowd was beginning to stir. A few places had their music on loud, and there were groups of men mostly sitting in rum shops along the way. Just after passing Albert and Fourth Street I arrived at my old house at 184 Albert Street. I had lived in that house for years with Granny, my guardian Retty Collins Greaves, who took care of my brother and me while my parents were in Essequibo. Granny Greaves and I were closer than she was with her own grandchildren, all of whom I knew and have remained close to even as we have gone off to distant places. Just beyond Granny's house on Albert Street I came across a decaying object that jogged my memory. It was ten foot by ten foot box with wooden siding and approximately three feet deep. It was partly overgrown and the wood was almost rotted away in one corner. It was a pit for people to throw their garbage in as they walked along the street, a relic of the era when people were urged keep the city clean and provided the means to do so. Albert Street was always a minor artery of the city with three or four corner stores along the twelve block stretch of road. It was a street that came alive three or four times a day and then quieted down. Every morning during the school year students from the East Coast would arrive by train and get off at the top of Vissengen and Albert and walk down *en-masse* to go to several high schools further along the way. It was also the route that several people took occasionally to get to their homes in

Queenstown. When St. Joseph's Girls High School moved from Charlestown it became even more popular as many of them began to use it to get there. Now the bungalows along the way have given way to a series of restaurants, open air rum shops and other commercial establishments turning it into a more commercial thoroughfare.

By the time dusk began to fall I was walking much faster and trying to get to my next destination. I was still gaping at the large new houses and transformation when I emerged through Sandman Place onto Brickdam. There was a wedding reception about to take place at the new fancy banquet hall at the corner opposite the Palms which attracted my attention and, even though I wanted to crash the affair for my own curiosity, my shirt was too sticky and I was too tired do so. I wanted to walk faster but could not for fear of sweating too much and making myself more uncomfortable. It was clear the humidity was rising. One block down Brickdam I could see my destination on Hadfield Street. The street lights came on as I rounded the corner. In the distance I could see my friend Horace Nurse on the bridge of his property. I increased my pace to not quite a trot hoping to surprise him but before I could get there he turned, went into the yard and closed the gate. "Don't you want me to come in?" I shouted from a distance. He seemed puzzled and cocked his head to find out if the comment was directed at him. As I came closer he remarked, "Oh it's you." Horace Nurse was Granny Graves's eldest grandchild. He, like so many of her other grandchildren, went to St. Stanislaus College. In school he was some five years my senior and never spoke to me. As a matter of fact he never even spoke to me when I visited his parents' home socially. Truth be told, Horace seldom spoke to anyone, even his classmates. To say he is a loner is an understatement. We became friends when I hired him to tutor me in mathematics. He was a teacher at Central High School awaiting a promised scholarship to study engineering in the

UK. Granny, like his parents were sweating together after his application was in and after he had his round of interviews. Granny was particularly excited because he would become the first person in her family to go to university. Her sister, Auntie Anna's daughter had by then graduated from University of West Indies (UWI). She was proud of her and talked of her quite often, but she wanted the same for her grandson. It was still a time when not many people had university degrees and not many scholarships were given to students, no matter how bright you were. When he was eventually chosen from many candidates the terms were stiff. His parents had to deposit the transport title for their house with the City Council. That was to make sure he returned to serve the City Council for two years. But one politician made an added side agreement; after calling Horace's father in for consultation he demanded that he pay his political party a nominal sum every month for the duration of the scholarship. It was an unfair burden that his father accepted under duress, but Granny was livid. Because of his love for his grandmother whom he visited every Sunday for brunch, and my constant presence in her house, our friendship continued throughout the years, through his marriage, the birth of his daughter Saran, and through his divorce. In fact, four months before my evening visit he had stayed with me for three weeks in my Riverside, Connecticut home to convalesce following an operation in NY. After leaving the City Council Horace worked in Africa for the UN and then for the government of Botswana before ending his career at the Caribbean Development Bank.

We sat in his garage facing the road in the same darkness and chatted for a while before moving inside. After talking for a while longer he called a taxi for me and I departed for my hotel. The charge was $1,500 Guyanese or $7 US. As soon as I opened the door of my hotel room I fell onto the bed, exhausted.

Two hours later I was up and out. I went to the hotel bar and then moved over to the dining room. There was a group of about twelve already there drinking and talking. I suspected they might be a group associated with me but I recognized no one. Sometime later Bunny Friemann came downstairs and joined the group. Within a few minutes thereafter the loudest person at that table came across and introduced himself to me. "Hi Burrowes yo rass down want to talk to we rass." It was my old friend Aubrey Kellawan. He took me to his table and introduced me to the others. Even though I did not recognize any of the people I was meeting I remembered their names distinctly. I had not seen or heard of them for forty nine years. The person at the table I knew best was Aubrey Kellawan. As a student in high school he was always friendly with everyone. He had a rare gift of making you feel you had his undivided attention no matter what you were talking about. His flat country drawl easily betrayed a seriousness underneath his ever-present smile. His was not an educated way of pronouncing words but, instead, it was a lazy way of speaking and very distinctive among us boys. At around 5'6" one hundred twenty pounds in his younger days, he always looked as though he could be blown over in a strong wind. He wore his personality with a careless ease. His head of wavy black hair and his distinct features pointed to his East Indian heritage. Yet if you met him walking down the street with his hands around the waist of a black woman and said, "Hi," he would stop you and exclaim, "Come, I want you to meet my cousin." This at a time when there was animosity or, at least, no love lost in the political competition between Indians and Blacks. Those quarrels had no effect on him as he maintained good relations with both. I did not recognize him earlier that evening because of his complete change in physical appearance. He wore his black and white hair at shoulder length and his corpulent size was not what I expected, but not even his moustache could hide his bright eyes. As soon as he spoke to me I knew who he was, he had not changed or modified his accent one iota. He was the same engaging and endearing personality. While the others jabbered away he leaned forward to me as though in confidence and explained that he was partly instrumental in starting the group comprising people who entered St. Stanislaus in 1959. So far they met every two years or so at a resort in Canada where most of them live. Apart from their ritual of eating, drinking and ribbing each other, they sponsored a St. Stanislaus student to go to the University of Guyana with the condition that upon completion he/she would return to teach there for two years. All they asked was that each member of our class contribute one hundred US dollars per year towards this cause. By the time I hit the sack later that evening I had had a full day.

EASTER

I got up at the crack of dawn with the sun streaming into my room. I could tell from the roar of the traffic that it was Sunday. The vehicles were travelling just as fast but there were far fewer of them whizzing by. I knew what I wanted to do once I was up that early; I wanted to go to church. I wanted to go to Our Lady of Fatima Church next to the Bourda cricket grounds. It was the church I attended throughout my youth and I had in mind to visit it again. The hotel called me a taxi and soon I was on my way. The early morning air was cool and, as the taxi flew down an empty highway, the breeze came rushing into the car making it even cooler. The driver, a young man in his late twenties, turned to me sitting in the front seat next to him and asked, "How do you like our country?"

It was not a question I wanted to answer since I had not seen enough to render any judgment but he looked at me with such expectation written all over his face that I had to answer. "It's great. With all of the new buildings and so on, the place looks great."

He went on to boast that Guyana was a great country, that if you worked hard and had a good plan you could realize your dream. He told me about his plans and emphasized how good things were. It was not the sort of conversation I wanted to have that early in the morning on my way to church but that decision was made for me once I sat in the front seat of his vehicle. I wondered where all his enthusiasm came from and asked if he ever wanted to go overseas, to the US or Canada or another Caribbean island. "I don't want to go to the US or any other country. We have a lot of opportunity here. All you have to do is work hard and not get distracted." He proceeded to tell me of the many different ways that a worker could become distracted from their goal. It was an early morning schooling I did not need but enjoyed nonetheless.

When we arrived at our destination I was startled there were no cars in evidence. Not a person around. I asked the taxi to wait in case I had to move on. After looking around and finding no one I thought I might be early for Mass. The church itself looked the same as I recalled, if just a bit worn, perhaps because it was built of concrete. I went around the back to the sacristy which was in desperate need of repair. Someone came to the door and said Mass was held the night before and there would be no Mass on Easter Sunday. I was sorely disappointed and returned to the car taking a moment to ponder what I wanted to do next. As I stood outside the car in the cool damp air of a lazy Sunday morning I kept looking around at the Bourda cricket grounds, the houses around and down Robb Street itself. I decided that because of the lack of traffic, it was a good time to ride around to see some parts of the city absent traffic or crowds. I had the driver take me along many of the streets I had been on before. Because Georgetown is not a very big city and because I did not want to engage the taxi for more time than was needed, my little excursion lasted only about half an hour driving slowly. I had the driver drop me off at Regent and Bourda Street so I could walk to my parents' house which was recently reclaimed by my brother Arthur.

Like me, neither my brother nor my mother had left Guyana with the intention of emigrating. Mother left when she got an invitation from my school to attend my graduation. Unbeknownst to me the school had sent her an invitation and she called to tell me she was coming to my graduation. I was surprised and asked, "Why?" in disbelief. I knew that my father's death a year earlier had thrown her into a tailspin but she had my two brothers to comfort her.

"How are you going to get a visa?" I asked. It was an open secret the US Embassy was limiting the number of visas issued to people from Guyana at that time because so many who were given tourist visas simply stayed. "Don't worry, I already got my visa," she replied, adding "I wasn't going to let an invitation like that go to waste." A smile flashed across my face when she said that. That's my mother, I thought. She travelled to the US with a simple suitcase leaving my brothers in the house. Within a year my brothers joined her, having obtained student visas themselves. The house and all its contents were more or less abandoned like so many others as people fled the country during a particularly difficult economic period. It fell to me to make arrangements about the house and I arranged for my friend Cynthia's sister, to stay in the house free of charge. This was predicated on the notion that some of us would return in a few years. Cynthia, Horace and their baby Saran took over the place and lived there with our furniture, wares, clothes etc. when her sister departed. When I returned to do research some years later they were still there. Our family friend, Commissioner of Police Henry Fraser, was about to retire and formed a company to manage properties like ours. He took over the task and has done so ever since. Apart from reviewing his semi-annual accounting I visit him every summer when he comes to New York to see his own children and I get a verbal report about the house.

I had the taxi driver drop me at the house Easter Sunday morning just around 10:00 am or so to see my brother Arthur and to examine the house more closely. Ours is one of the few houses that remain on stilts some twelve feet high since Georgetown is three to five feet below sea level. I felt it needed to stay that way, and over the years I have resisted the pressure to add an apartment at ground level "like everyone else". The house itself needed some care, a good coat of paint and some updating. I was greeted at the entrance to the rental property in the rear by some fifteen chickens and two noisy barking dogs. My brother Arthur was still away for the long weekend. At the rear of the yard the galvanized fence was broken and needed fixing so I peered over to see the state of the alley that runs at the back which supplies drainage, and is usually kept up by the Town Council. The grass was overgrown, the gutters silted up and clearly posing a health hazard where mosquitoes and other unwanted pests could breed. The incessant yapping of the dogs woke up the tenant who shared the house in the rear. Cornell Greaves had lived in the apartment since my mother rented it to him nearly forty years ago. He explained that the personal stuff I stored in a room next to his apartment was moved out some time ago because most of it had crumbled to dust.

As I was exiting the rear of the house the lady in the front called out to me from the rear kitchen door. She beckoned me to come up the front steps and not use the rear as I was attempting to do. I learned she was a freelance TV and print journalist. She kept the inside of the old place in immaculate condition and encouraged me to visit each room, my old bedroom, my parents' bedroom, the kitchen and the bathroom. It was funny to see that the gas range my father bought from William Fogarty's store all those years ago was still in use. The rest of our furnishings were gone, thrown away or carted off by different tenants. She delighted in telling me about herself and her work, and about what she had done to make the place and her surroundings more pleasant and livable. She drew my attention to the flowers she had planted outside and the fact that she kept the gutters in front clean of silt or debris. She complained about the large four story buildings going up opposite, and the mess the contractors made with no interest in cleaning it up because of a lack of inspectors. Over the years the rent had gone to maintaining the house. But houses do need a major renovation from time to time and ours had not had one. As I was learning the property lay smack in the middle of a thriving business district and looked out of place. A decision needed to be made.

I left the house and walked around the corner to Bourda Market. A commotion of stalls greeted me as I got thirty yards beyond Regent Street. There were people calling to me through the thick crowd offering to show me what they were selling. I stopped at the stall of one lady to see her mangoes and other fruits. She said business was good but she complained about the daily fees she and other stall workers had to pay despite the fact that stalls were in poor condition. It was obvious that while the city Council was collecting a fee from the hucksters they had made no attempt to bring some organization or symmetry to make shopping there more pleasant or profitable.

In the market itself many of the stalls were just beginning to open. All around there were people calling to passers-by anxious to show what they had for sale. The concrete underfoot was so worn down there were indentations that made walking tricky. I walked past the pharmacy area and found myself where the butchers were, in a dark, dingy and decaying building. As I was making my way out of the market I realized a strange smell permeated the air. I thought it must be coming from the fish mongers area I was approaching. A woman and her young son were manning this stall. The child, about 12 years old, was diligently cleaning a fish as his mother spoke to me. She said she did not detect any unusual smell in the area. I suddenly realized the smell was coming from bathrooms which were in a state of disrepair. Although they had clearly been cleaned, no disinfectant or air freshener had been used.

Outside the market once again I wound my way through fruit and vegetable stands. Standing in a pharmacy on a side street and talking to the person behind the counter was a woman and her significant other who were asking for medicine for her sick baby. She described the ailment and the pharmacist recommended something but said she had to buy a syringe to administer the medication. The worry in the woman's voice was evident as she asked several more questions but, eventually, her boyfriend pulled out a wad of cash and paid for everything. I wanted to ask them about the wisdom of their actions and why she didn't take the baby to the hospital ER, but I couldn't. I realized this is how people on the edge live. I continued past the SPCA and returned to Regent Street. In front of the Bourda Post Office two letter boxes from the colonial era still stood. Made from cast iron with "Royal Mail" lettering stamped at the top, both boxes were painted red and were rotting from the bottom up, just for want of a new concrete base and a little care. I walked up a few blocks and decided to go past my house on Charlotte Street once again. On my way there, on Bourda Street, the stalls I had passed before and barely noticed because they had been closed were now open. I passed a few stalls selling dresses and then came to a freshly painted and well put together "Georgetown Famous Shoe Store." The stall was much better kept than the others and its name cried out for recognition. The owner, a woman in her mid-forties, was dressed in tight fitting clothes and seemed a bit bored as I approached her. She said she owned her store for ten years and travelled to the US once or twice a year when she needed to restock. When I asked her why she did not stay in the US where she could make a more certain wage for her and her family she dismissed my suggestion as absurd. Frankly I was surprised at her response. "I have a good life here, I like it and I do okay." I asked, "How do you get a US visa to go there so often?" She was once again a little indignant at my question and replied, "A US visa isn't hard to get. Everyone who wants one gets one." She explained that the US Embassy gives visas to people like her readily because they know we are traders who travel there to buy merchandise for resale. She explained that years ago, the Embassy gave people problems but that was no longer the case. She was one of thousands of people from the Caribbean and elsewhere who travelled there so frequently. In fact, she explained that, now, the shoe was on the other foot: US merchants relied on them to purchase out-of-fashion garments and shoes so they could take more risk up front and not worry as much about overstocking. She had met many people from Latin America who did the same thing she did so they told each other where to get merchandise, and they all were aware that if the Americans cut out their visas they could find somewhere else to make their purchases. I made a comment to the effect that the US was the capital of the garment trading business so she was dependent on them and she promptly informed me I didn't know what I was talking about! "Brazil is a big shoe manufacturer," she shot back, and she could get her shop filled there, "and they are doing garments now too. They are dying for us to go there to do our shopping. We don't need America, America needs us more. It's not like the old days you know. We have choices now."

As we talked a customer would pass by and inquire about the price of something. Without hesitating she would look at the customer, look at the item and give a price or answer a question. I was impressed with her business savvy so I asked her name. "My name is Ingrid McRae. Why?" I got goose bumps. I look at her broad face and big brown eyes more closely. "My grandmother's name was McRae," I replied still thinking of the coincidence. I spent the rest of the time trying to establish whether we were related or not, but both of us had such sketchy information about our past that we let it go and just said goodbye. It was surreal talking to her about business and then ending with the possibility we could well be related. The resemblance to Grandmother's family was there.

I walked past my house as I had intended and at the corner I saw a sight I could not believe. There at the corner of Charlotte and Alexander Street surviving among the great building boom that is Georgetown was a genuine "range house", the city's version of a "logie", the slave and indentured servants' dwelling found on the sugar estates. The city version, like the one I was staring at 207 Alexander Street in Lacy Town, stood two to three feet off the ground. It was about sixty feet long and ten feet wide, and was divided into four one room apartments. The first apartment had no stairs so that the renter had to hop up to get into his dwelling. The second apartment was occupied by a woman in her mid-sixties who had lived there for many years. She was bemused that her simple dwelling, built when slaves were first settled into Georgetown and used until the 1950's as entry level rentals for people coming in from distant villages, was of interest to me. The yard itself was cleaner than most in the area, which did not make it seem as rundown as some of the other buildings I had seen.

It was just after midday by then and the blue sky was filled with a pleasant sunshine. The temperature was a breezy eighty degrees and a light wind gave the day an easy feel. Despite that, however, I felt a bit tired. I suppose I was like a child who was burning up with excitement so incessantly that I felt I had to rest. I hailed a cab back to my hotel to relax and rejuvenate. As I sat in the front seat of the taxi, I asked the driver to turn off the air conditioner. I rolled down the window and allowed the rushing breeze to pound my face. As we approached a sign I had passed every time I travelled the East Coast Highway leading to my hotel, I asked the driver to pull in and take me through Courida Park, an ocean-front development. I had suspected as I passed the sign several times before that it was the suburban development I had secretly marked down in my mind as the place I wanted to live in when I returned to Guyana. The trouble was, after not thinking about it for so many decades, I could not remember its name when I wanted to years later. It had remained the same tranquil development it had always been. A few houses had been enlarged and others dismantled for bigger dwellings. I came upon two dwellings next to each other, both unoccupied, both seemed to have no furniture and both needed a good coat of paint to fall in with the neighbors. I assumed they belonged to some family that had gone abroad and still wanted to maintain a foothold in their homeland. Down another street, a massive new house was under construction. By my calculation it must have been near six thousand square feet. My exclamation caused the driver to say, "Let me show you an even bigger one a little ways over." It was another huge three-story structure that dwarfed everything around it. Driving through Courida Park I realized that even before I left Guyana, the new suburbs outside of the city of Georgetown were already being constructed purely of concrete, and that it was I who had failed to see where the future was going.

I must have been in my room for a half an hour when the telephone rang. "Your cousin is downstairs. Should I send him up or are you going to come down?" "Send him up."

I was at a loss to know which cousin it was. I had written letters to a few people, family and friends, that I would be back and where I would be staying. Interestingly, no one had called or dropped by until then. When I opened the door I knew immediately who it was. The man standing in front of my door was Aubrey Burrowes, the son of my Uncle Jack, a spitting image of him. We hugged after not seeing each other since we were teens. He was five feet eleven, very dark in complexion with long dreadlocks. I could tell by looking at him he was about 130 lbs fully dressed that he did not have an ounce of fat on his body. Aubrey said he was then sixty years old. His wife, like mine, had also died from cancer within a year of being diagnosed. His daughter was married with two children, his son, a plumber, still lived with him in his family's house, and his youngest daughter was with her grandmother in Brooklyn,

New York. I was lying on the bed propped up by two pillows as we chatted and he sat in the chair just near the door. I felt a little sad that I did not get to know my cousin but I felt a bit better when he said, "We get all your cards and now that I live in the house I tell Greta and Esme that you wrote and what you say." At least they knew I made an effort to keep my link with them. I was pleased a lot that he was in touch with Uncle Harold's daughter Esme and informed her about me. For thirty years I had sent my uncle a card every Christmas, and because in all that time I never received a reply, I never knew what happened until I received a phone call one day some eleven years ago from his sister Colleen. She and her family were transferred to the US with the Salvation Army and she used the telephone number I had sent every year in my card to get in touch with me.

My cousin Arnold and I chatted for a long time. There were periods of silence during which we had nothing to say, but I was just delighted to lie there and watch him. I asked about Uncle Sidney's house "over the river", because I could not remember the name of the village in which he lived. "Denamstel," he reminded me. "Yes, Denamstel," I repeated hoping to commit it to memory for a few more years. He explained the house was left to his family and now belonged to his son. I was glad to hear that the property of my childless uncle had remained in the family. He seemed pleased I remembered him, and when I augmented my memory with other incidents he smiled broadly, showing a mouth filled with pearly white teeth. It was with mixed feelings that he rose and said goodbye. "How did you get here?" I asked. "By bus," he answered. I was deeply moved that this poor man, my dear cousin, had taken the time and spent part of his meagre resources to travel outside the city to come to see me.

As soon as my cousin left I had to dash downstairs to meet the others who had by then assembled to attend a welcome party for our high school class of '59. Peter Headecker, a classmate, motioned to me to join him and his family. Frankly, I did not recognize Peter when we were first introduced the evening before. What I did remember, however, was his distinctive name. Bernard Friemann had sent me several e-mails of those who had indicated an interest in journeying to Guyana for the event. I had wondered about several of the names from time to time and his was one. I was glad Peter automatically included me so I was sure of getting to the affair. He and his wife Bonnie had called a minibus for their large party. As soon as we took off it was interesting to listen to their comments about the road and houses as we travelled along the highway. As everyone was commenting about the houses and scenery Bunny asked Peter a question about his mother which I missed. When Peter replied that his mother had not been quite the same since the accident in which one of the sisters was killed, I automatically remembered who he was, where he lived, and his family. A man of average height and build, he has maintained a youthful figure and an easygoing personality. His grey hair and narrow-set eyes masked a determined personality that could assess a person and situation quickly. Those qualities made him an enormously successful sight engineer in his adopted Canada. Just as we turned off the highway a dispute broke out in the van as to what our destination was. "Is it Bel Air Gardens, or Bel Air Park?" someone asked. A discussion ensued in our van. I gave the driver the letter Bunny left me with the address and simply refrained from participating. My attitude was to let them figure it out so I could enjoy the scenery. We overshot the turn-off and had to reverse down the street. The houses in Bel Air Gardens were mostly built before we all left Guyana. They were all built of concrete, extremely well kept and there was no garbage in the road or in the gutters. We could have been in any suburb anywhere in the world. Suddenly we realized we were lost in the winding road that branched off and turned into one with another name. While trying to locate our position we ran into a taxi carrying Bunny Friemann, Dale and Colin Morgan. They, too, were lost but Bunny was on his phone to our hosts so we simply followed his taxi.

Within a minute or so we arrived at our destination. As we approached the high gate, a large overweight African Guyanese woman dressed in dark pants and a white shirt, and wearing the insignia of a security service rose from her seat and came to the gate. Words were exchanged and the electric gate retracted to let us in. The home was that of the regional manager of a Canadian bank and cousin of our classmate Peter St. Aubyn. The place was in impeccable condition. Several kinds of orchids and other potted plants lined the short driveway as we entered. The guard box for the security guard was tucked neatly in the back next to the garage. The whole approach to the house was done in concrete and was spotlessly clean. We walked up a narrow concrete path with a slight incline lined with many more tropical flowers, which led to a cabana overlooking a swimming pool. The grounds surrounding the pool were not extensive, but every blade of grass had been carefully cut to fit the uniform look of suburbs everywhere. In the cabana the hosts, Mr. & Mrs. St. Aubyn greeted us. They had set up one table with liquor of every type and another with hors d'oeuvres. A few of our classmates had already arrived. Aubrey Kellawan, who was already there with his wife, was holding court, his shoulder length greying hair blowing in the gentle breeze. Our hosts were dutifully urging us to get a drink even before we had fully taken in the atmosphere. Cyril DaSilva, another classmate, was behind the bar ministering to his own needs and Peter St. Aubyn stood there with a glass in hand looking exactly as I remembered him. Peter was a man with a perpetual smile who always looked as though he had just pulled off a prank of some sort and was waiting to be found out. His face maintained a youthful look despite his middle-age paunch. Cyril DaSilva who seemed to be his comrade-in-arms had become stocky but carried his weight with apparent ease. They both looked younger than I knew they were, and their wives seemed to be the perfect complements to their personalities knowing when to restrain their exuberance without being obvious.

Randy Bradford came walking up greeting everyone like a politician, shaking hands, back slapping. As Dale was fond of saying, "Braddy is still Braddy," meaning that he is still the same larger than life fellow he was in high school. He is fully grey with thinning hair and a thick moustache. The gap in his front teeth which had always marked him has become slightly wider thus emphasizing the deep lines around his eyes and mouth. He is a stocky man who walks with a slight stoop that is noticeable when he stands. When he speaks his dark penetrating eyes come alive and his restless energy begins to show. He is a man of reflection and always an engaging person. I had remembered Randy Bradford as, simply put, the brightest boy in our class. What distinguished him was that he knew it and insisted he be recognized among those who would challenge him or doubt his ability. In a Jesuit high school known for its humility and understatement he always showed that was not his game. Since I did not even figure as part of his competition he was always friendly and kind to me, a side of him the others seldom saw. I had just finished taking in Bradford's entry and was still chatting with Andy Yansen, the only other American besides Bunny and me, when another commotion ensued.

John Carpenter had arrived. John and his wife were our official hosts while in Guyana. Everyone except me had seen him since we were in school together. In the interim he had attended Cornell in the US on a food technology scholarship. He had absolutely no interest in the subject but majored in it to satisfy the terms he had agreed to, all to get an education from a fine institution. Afterwards, he returned to Guyana and became a businessman but still travelled to Toronto, Canada every year to get his medical checkup and to see friends including the '59ers. He had become so successful in business that even my taxi driver knew him, and would tell me that Johnny Carpenter is "one of those guys who knows this country. He knows every stitch of the interior and everything that's going on." Bunny had alerted me to Carpy's success months ago but it was a joy to see him in the flesh after some 45 years.

John Carpenter had always been a friend of mine. He and Bunny Friemann were the only two people who consistently debated me over politics sometimes riding around on our bicycles often ending up at their "bottom house" a small area under the stilts. I had presumed for a long time that he had returned to his father's country, the UK, or to Canada as many others did. I was pleasantly astonished when Bunny told me he had been in Guyana all this time. As he approached with his wife next to him John kept saying as he greeted us, "I've got to get a drink." So he moved directly to the bar, deciding what to drink, and went over to greet a number of wives who were all sitting on one side of the cabana. Carpy was still the same happy person I remembered. He cut a handsome picture with his slim neatly trimmed beard and moustache, and his full head of greying hair. He wore shorts and a polo shirt and seemed to command the conversation as he moved from group to group, sometimes shouting over the heads of the group he was with to another sharing stories about our past. It turned out that John Carpenter had become an able story teller with a good memory for things we did at school. Not only that, but over the years he had become so plugged into the affairs of Guyana that he had an encyclopedic knowledge of the players and their positions. His incisive analysis of several events elucidated why he had become so successful. It was clear he was a man of confidence and poise who, while shaped by his surroundings, had not been defined by them. He had even become something of a comedian with the ability to give a comical spin along with a serious reply to a political matter. Throughout the evening he moved around with a certain territorial ease that suggested he was totally comfortable with the life he was living.

Carpy's arrival was so dramatic that I did not see Romeo Periera and his wife come in. As with Peter Headecker, I could not place Romeo but always remembered his name. He had become a successful business man also but, unlike Carpy, did not have nor seem to want any cheerleaders on his team. He had remained the same shy person I remembered. A reserved man, bald with glasses, he exuded an air that said, "I know who I am, I don't need anyone to tell me." His wife was a woman of understated elegance.

I was walking around taking in the scene when I spotted a profile I would know anywhere. It was Norman Nig-A-Qui. He and I were friends in school and often hung out with the same people in front of Reagan Miller's house on Anaira Street. It was a group that included classmates Andy Yansen and Cyril Rodriques. Nippy, as everyone called him for short, was always a very disciplined fellow. We would be talking about the events of the day or about what we saw coming in the future when he would announce, "I've got to go. I gotta do my homework." I never went to his house or knew where he lived but he was always friendly, if a little mysterious. Not because he was evasive or secretive but because his replies were terse and his inquiries few. I knew he left to study in the US at Howard University in Washington DC where a lot of Guyanese went to study at that time. Many years later a mutual friend told me Nippy had returned to work with Guyana's government for two years or so and then went back to the US. As I approached I could see Nippy had not changed one bit. Standing there in his three quarter length trousers and flowing collared shirt, he was about the same weight as in high school. His hair line was the same except his hair was white and, set against his bronze skin it gave him a healthy look. It appeared Norman had maintained the rigorous discipline of his youth throughout his life. He said after leaving Howard University he pursued graduate work at Perdue and then went to work in Colorado. He had never officially left home as he returned regularly over the years to see his and his wife's family. His daughter was a graduate of the US Air Force Academy and flew fighter jets. His son had credentials all his own. He was proud of them as he pulled out his i-phone to show me pictures. With his children established, he and his wife had returned to live in Guyana permanently and had bought a place up the East Coast. It was clear to me he felt happy and fulfilled.

I returned from speaking to Norman Nig-A-Qui next to the pool and joined the cluster around Carpy. Just then he rose and shouted, "Everyone please gather around." It took a few seconds for people having a good time to do so and St. Aubyn tried to make a few jokes in the meantime, but his wife arrived at his side just in time to hold him in check. John Carpenter welcomed us and told us what was planned for the days ahead. He said the most important part of our meeting as far as he was concerned was the obligation we had undertaken to put one student through university. He went on to say we were lucky since the very first student we sponsored, who was now in her third year, was "a dream to work with". He described her as bright, dedicated, hardworking. The adjectives just flowed in praising her. "What is her major?" shouted Cyril DaSilva. "You haven't told us what her major is," chimed in St. Aubyn, his wife tugging at his shirt sleeve. "She is a chemistry major, a wonderful person to work with. You can't believe how lucky we are." He confirmed that she would be obliged, as a condition of our sponsorship to return to our alma mater to teach for two years. "I would really like to see her get a scholarship or for us to sponsor her to do a master's degree after she is finished."

The introduction of this new idea, while many years in the future, brought a flurry of questions and opinions about whether someone else should be given an opportunity versus relying on one student. Again Carpenter mentioned he wanted to do something for her after she graduated and completed her two years of teaching. John Carpenter used the word "lucky" about the scholarship student so many times, and was so passionate in advocating on her behalf that I got the feeling he would move heaven and earth for her to go on. He also gave recognition to Aubrey Kellawan as the person who had patched the group together and sustained it in Canada. He thanked him for his work and for the fact that we were not only a drinking club but we had added a progressive social component to our charter. By this time Carpy was on his third or fourth drink and he was just getting started. So after getting yet another drink he sat down among us to reminisce.

He and St. Aubyn recalled the time St. Aubyn was late arriving at his house which made them both late for school. Once they reached school the principal, Father John Hopkinson, spotted the late-comers and gave Carpy detention. They all had a good laugh that Carpy was the only prefect ever to get detention. In the midst of reminiscing he turned to me still doubled over in laughter over something that was said and remarked, "Don't think I forgot we used to call you Burro-goat." To which Andy Yansen replied with a chuckle, "I was wondering when someone would remember that." A number of people chuckled also, as did I. The barb directed at me did not engender further comments either because of politeness or faded memory. Most of the memories we shared of St. Stanislaus were about the masters who taught us. Dale Morgan remembered Stanley Marks as a drill sergeant of a Latin teacher, and the time his balls fell out of his shorts while getting a ball at "Big Grounds". St. Aubyn and Cyril DaSilva remembered their encounters with Father Darke. The person who brought almost universal acclaim was Father Maxwell. He was the resident technologist and tinkerer. He encouraged his students to build transistor radios and all sorts of contraptions. I remembered Father Maxwell for another reason. He was my English teacher and, at the end of every class, he would give us a dozen or so words and their definitions to remember. As the term came to a close his list grew longer and longer. This learning exercise served me so well that, even today, I continue to recall and use many of those words with great ease. Whether it was because of his attitude or because he was a good teacher I found it interesting that there was so much agreement about the impact Father Maxwell had on our lives.

When the talk turned to Father Lynch (Jiggo), the mathematics teacher, Dale Morgan was full of stories. His teaching style was typical of British teachers at the time. They guided you but seldom taught you anything. Especially for the boys in sixth form. Under this system only the truly gifted and the well prepared ever succeeded. Not that Father Lynch did not know his stuff. When everyone was stumped he would approach the blackboard and, like a magician, work out the answer with ease. Dale took great pride in telling us before Randy Bradford arrived that, one Saturday morning, Father Lynch summoned his students to a math exam. Randy Bradford arrived seconds before the test was due to start. He read the problems, put his foot on the desk and stared out the window. An hour passed and Bradford was in the same position while the other students worked feverishly at their problems. When about half the time had elapsed Bradford read the problem once again, began working on it and finished along with all the other students. He also recalled that Father Lynch entered the classroom one day and informed the students that the US embassy wanted them to take "some exam the Americans have concocted, some nonsense," he said with disdain, since they were contemplating giving scholarships to US universities. He assured them, "You should all do well." The Saturday of that week all the students took the exam and no one got less than seven hundred out of 800 in Math or English. Many of our teachers were British and most of them had a disdain for institutions that were not British. Their students, however, who were anxious for a college education could not afford to share their point of view, as the British government offered only one scholarship to Guyana per year as they did in many of their colonies.

Our conversations ranged from memories of school to talking about the difficulties some people had in getting jobs in Canada when many of them arrived in the late '60s. A few people described the tactics used by Canadian employers to deny them jobs by insisting they have Canadian experience. None of the guys were bitter, but they lamented having to jump through hoops to get the jobs for which they had experience and were readily available. Their recollection got a spirited response from John Carpenter. He said he especially disliked the Canadian government and went on to give a number of reasons why. This even though he regularly went to Canada for medical check-ups and so on. He was equally spirited about the US. "I hate the American government. The trouble with Americans is that they can't take a joke." As he went on to elaborate I wondered why such a prominent businessman so disliked both the US and Canada. Whether he was frustrated by the rules for travel or something else I could not discern.

Dusk had begun to fall, a signal that the time to leave was approaching. Once again John Carpenter took charge. By this time he was little tipsy. I told him he should not drive so he arranged for each person who had arrived by taxi to be driven home or to some place convenient. Dale, his son Colin, Bunny and I had decided to go to the New Thriving restaurant for dinner and Romeo Pereira and his wife drove us there, but left. As soon as we were seated we were joined by Karyl Arthur who everyone called "KK". He had arrived midway through the party in Bel Air and everyone seemed to know him well except me. He was a slim man of around five feet five with a full beard and glasses. KK was a professor of engineering at the University of Guyana. He looked and sounded like a nerd, but I was glad he decided to join us for dinner. We ordered our entrées, and had just began to enjoy our meal at what was clearly the hottest new restaurant in the city when Romeo and Barbara Pereira returned and asked to join us too. She said they had driven a few blocks when they decided they did not want to go home and start cooking dinner. Just as we were about finished eating, Norman Nig-A-Qui and Andy Yansen arrived to get take-out from the restaurant and joined us at our table for our upscale Chinese dinner. At the end of our meal we bade each other farewell as a number of taxi drivers approached asking for our destinations. Bunny and I were the only two who needed a taxi. I stepped in front of him and thought I would try something. "We are going to Grand Coastal and I am willing to pay twelve hundred." "The charge for Grand Coastal is 1500" replied one driver. "I am willing to pay 1200," I repeated. "It is late you are all looking for customers." "So you are telling us how much to charge?" chimed in someone else. "OK I will do it for twelve hundred," said a heavy set driver dressed in dark trousers and a white shirt. Bunny and I got into his car and he took off like the proverbial "bat out of hell". Within a few minutes we found ourselves sailing through the city at a high speed since it was Sunday night and the traffic was light. As soon as we hit the East Coast Highway the driver's speed increased. Sixty, seventy, seventy-five mph; it was a reckless speed for such a highway. Bunny and I, both speechless from the time we took off looked at each other. "I think you had better slow down a little," I said to the driver. One of us asked him a question hoping he would slow down to give us the answer but he continued on. When he weaved past one car and then another, I knew he was out of control. We did not have our seat belts on and I could not risk looking for one. I just held on to the hand rail, braced myself and kept my eyes peeled to the road, not taking in the scenery as I usually did. When we pulled into the hotel driveway Bunny emerged from the car exclaiming, "Thank God we got here alive. I was wondering whether we would make it."

The ride was a harrowing twenty minute experience. As I gave the driver his fare I said, "You are a bad driver. You might think you are a good driver but you are not. You were out of control." I am not certain my words made a difference but I felt I had to say something. At the end of the ride I did not feel so smart about trying to negotiate a cheaper price for the trip.

After staying in my room for a while I went downstairs to the bar where people were watching cricket on ESPN. On another screen nearby they were watching English Champion League soccer. I had no idea ESPN covered cricket but the barman assured me they did. I asked him about NCAA or American Basketball and he told me I could access that through the TV in my room. He realized I did not know how to operate the TV properly so he promised to send someone up to help me. I fell asleep watching TV.

EASTER 2

Just about at the break of dawn, a little after 5:00 am, the electricity flickered on and off twice for ten or twenty seconds. I was lying in bed waiting for a complete shutdown but it never came. I was too cold from the powerful air conditioner in the room to get up and turn it off. I finally got out of bed at 7:30 or so and began to write. Sometime later I took a break and called my cousin Esme to let her know I planned to drop by and see her at some point. Esme sounded grouchy when she answered the telephone so I was sorry I had called that early but she perked up when she heard my voice and said she was up but resting. I then called my cousin Greta Burrowes McDonald and arranged to meet at her office downtown. Even though by then I had turned off the air conditioner, the room was so cold I took a hurried shower and went downstairs to try to get warm. As soon as I left the room my glasses fogged up so I had to stand at the top of the stairs and wipe them off before descending.

Upon entering the huge dining room I saw Peter Headecker sitting at a long table with his large party in tow. Also at the table was Bunny Friemann and, lo and behold, Mark McWatt. Once again before I could decide what to do Peter rose from his position at the head of the table and pulled a chair from a table nearby bidding me to join them. I was glad I did not have to ask but was made so welcome into what was for him a family holiday of discovery. Peter had travelled to our reunion with his wife Bonny Fung Headecker, his daughter Tina and her husband

Paul, his son Daniel and Daniel's girlfriend, none of whom had visited Guyana before. Bonnie had not seen Guyana since she left for the University of New Brunswick. Once she decided to accompany her husband Peter, her sister Dohne Fung, a former Guyana scholar living in England and her brother, Derek Fung living in Canada all decided to make it a family visit. Peter had a big brood to worry about and yet, from the time we first met, he kept inviting me to join them. I was grateful he did so every time as it saved my having to ask. Everyone in his family seemed to follow his lead. At the table on Easter Monday morning everyone was already having breakfast while Bunny Friemann and Mark McWatt had just ordered theirs. Bunny looked especially happy because he had looked forward to seeing Mark from the time he began planning to attend the reunion and had arranged for them to room together. He had first expected Mark to arrive on Friday, then on Saturday and seemed happy when he finally arrived on Sunday night.

For my money Mark McWatt was simply the brightest boy in our class, a teacher's pet without wanting that accolade. He always knew his schoolwork because he studied hard and he participated in school debates and was a member of the Boy Scouts. He was always humble and willing to take a minute to talk with others who were not as smart as he was. Throughout my years as a student he was always a role model for me. Every time I was told I was good along the way, I would think, "If you guys think I am good, you should see the people I went to school with," and Mark's image would flash in my mind. I knew from his father that Mark had gone to school in Canada, and to the University of Leeds to do graduate work. It was not until I re-established contact with Bunny Friemann that I found out he had returned to the Caribbean and had become an English professor at the University of the West Indies Cave Hill campus in Barbados, and had won several prizes for his poetry and short stories. Bunny had, I suspected, read all of his output.

As soon as I sat at the table Mark told me he was having the "salt fish and bake" and urged me to do the same. I proudly and loudly announced how much I admired him and how many times I thought of him over the years. He seemed a little amused, embarrassed and hastened to make light of my remarks. He was genuinely pleased to be among us and was eager to know what had transpired so far. I was glad to see he had not changed.

The conversation at the table turned to the minor travel problems some had at the Grand Coastal and elsewhere. Bernard Friemann was fixated for several days on the fact that the safe in his room did not work properly. Hotel personnel eventually put in a new one for him. Then Peter and Bonnie talked about their experiences. Peter began a story and Bonnie finished it about a malfunction of hotel room equipment in Florida and other hotel issues in Thailand. I could see from their conversation that Peter was more accepting and was inclined to make the best of bad situations while Bonnie found these inconveniences irritating while on holiday. Bonnie and I got into an exchange over her dislike for Thailand because of its hovels, crowds, heat and general congestion. I surmised from her comments that she had been brought up in very sheltered surroundings, standard for many girls in her era. In many cases all they were asked to do was study and ignore all else. I suspect they were absolved from doing housework, shielded from bad news, and told where they could go and even to whom they could speak. Bonnie, however, left the sheltered life she led in Guyana and went off to Canada where she appeared to have lived in one bucolic setting after another. She told me it was the second go- around for both Peter and her and described the drama that surrounded their first meeting. I could tell as we continued to speak, that she was a very bright woman who was careful not to show off.

As we broke up into little groups chatting at the same table, the conversation returned to one central subject. Why did the people of Guyana take kite flying on Easter Monday so seriously? Everyone had an opinion but no one could say why. We all agreed it was the one event we truly missed and wanted to re-connect with when we went to our second engagement in a few hours.

It was a bright, sunny and increasingly warm day as we departed. We boarded our respective vans and set out for a picnic John Carpenter had arranged for us at what was known as "Big Ground" among us boys from St. Stanislaus. We travelled along the East Coast Highway onto Clive Lloyd Drive and then onto Carifesta Avenue, essentially the same road but with different names along the way. We arrived at our destination to see John patiently waiting under a tent he had erected with five kites laying on the table. Romeo and Barbara Periera, Dale and Colin Morgan, Peter St. Aubyn and his wife, Aubrey Kellawan and his wife, Andy Yansen and I were all sitting in a sort of a semi-circle when some people began asking John Carpenter about mutual friends. The table with the liquor was being set up as Carpy spoke. Someone shouted out to him, "What are you drinking Carpy?" "Nothing for me, I am not drinking today. Boy you don't know what happened to me yesterday." He went on to explain that he did not know how much he had to drink the day before and became frightened by that lapse. He confessed he did not do so often but he thought seeing us made him drink much more than was usual. He said he actually threw up when he got home but did so quietly out of earshot of his wife because she was already angry with him for over indulging. He added that customarily he did not drink during Lent. He seemed shaken as he told the story glancing occasionally over to his left where his wife was sitting.

The conversation turned nostalgic which changed the mood immediately. Dale Morgan recalled that, in the early days of passenger planes coming to Guyana, extended families would travel to the airport in a caravan to see their loved one off. Many of them often dressed for the occasion. Once they arrived at the ramshackle building, many of them would cry because they feared they might never see their loved one again. "You would think the person died or something." "There is no difference between someone leaving for good and dying," came a rejoinder from Mark McWatt.

Shortly afterwards, John Carpenter ducked out of the tent under which we were all sitting and began to raise the first kite. The kite soared in the wind but pitched wildly from side to side. "Needs more tail," went up a cry almost in unison. Carpy searched around and found some dry bark of a tree. The kite looked a sight as it struggled to stay aloft with such an unnatural appendage. He found two other objects which met with the same result. For a little while Carpy looked desperate. Here he had five kites, and no extra tail. Most seasoned kite fliers know you have to have extra tail and he clearly had forgotten. The trouble was that kite flying was one of the main reasons many people chose Easter to visit and he wanted to put on a good show. Someone saved the day when some tail was found and, once attached, the kite rose and flew majestically over the field. After the kite held its position aloft for a few minutes Carpy handed it over to Colin Morgan and began to get another one up. It was just as much fun seeing Carpy struggle to get the second kite up when Peter Headecker's son-in-law began to get a third kite up on his own. He and his brother-in-law Daniel raised theirs in no time. By this time a number of people were raising their kites in the adjoining field and along the seawall in the distance.

With Colin enjoying himself Dale turned to us to report almost gleefully that he had gone to visit some distant relatives who he had not seen since he was twelve years old. They greeted him with such enthusiasm that he was overwhelmed and filled with pride. They not only welcomed him, but they filled in several gaps in his knowledge of his family tree and introduced him to some relatives he did not know existed. They all wanted him and Colin to join them for dinner and to spend time with them. He was touched by their response and more so because his son was with him. He clearly wanted Colin to know that he had relatives who would welcome him and care for him if need be since he had grown up in the US as an only child with immigrant parents, and not much family around to anchor him. Standing in the field looking skywards with his full head of shaggy hair and a smile on his face Colin seemed to be enjoying himself.

There was a lot of liquor in the back of the tent and very few people seemed to be drinking. The sun overhead was beating down on us. The humidity was up even though we were sitting just two hundred yards away from the wide Atlantic Ocean. Water seemed to be the preferred beverage of the day. A few of us wanted to wander off for a walk on the sea wall but could not do so because the old entrance to the grounds we once used from Sea-wall Road was cut off and completely replaced with the present one on Carifesta Avenue. Since we could not go up to the wall we settled for conversation instead. We began to debate where the original bridge was and what the earth dam now called Carifesta Avenue was like. Norman Nig-A-Qui observed out loud that the young people were sitting at the back of the tent "looking at us old people." Carpy was trying to get another kite up and Bonnie noted, "It's a Chinese kite." "Do you want me to put it up for you?" chimed in someone else.

"Do you need a pure Chinese or a mongrel Chinese?" asked Bonnie standing at the entrance of the tent with a glass of water in her hand. She looked out at the wide expanse of field that we few had to ourselves. There in the middle of the field was her sister lying on her back flying a kite and looking up at the blue sky. She had been lying there in that passive position for more than a half an hour alone with her thoughts. Then Bonnie said, "Look at my sister. She is flying a kite in her sandals and socks; she's so English." With that she walked towards her, glass in hand, and offered her sister a glass of water. Dohne sat up under her floppy English gardener's hat, drank a glass of water then went back to her original position.

Once Carpy sat down he seemed relieved that he managed to get the kites up. Just then KK arrived carrying a cooler of some size filled with ice. It was a sight to see a man of his slight build get the cooler to where we were all camped at the other side of the field. Once the kites were in the air the conversation in our tent resumed. At some point while talking and looking at the increasing numbers of kites around Tina Headecker Trebilco remarked, "The taxi driver said he will have to dodge all of the kites flying and landing on the road." "And the fun is to drive all over them when they fall and ruin all their fun," replied Carpy. It was these comments that caused Bunny Freimann to remark much later, "Who would have thought that, of all of us, Carpy would emerge as the extrovert."

A massive army truck arrived at the gate bringing our catered lunch. After we were told what the large olive green vehicle making its way in was carrying, a surprised Peter Headecker said, "They bring it in an army truck?" "Should we hide?" asked Bonnie. "No that is how our caterers take stuff into the interior, so they use the trucks sometimes around the city also," Carpy explained. It was probably in counting to make sure enough box lunches were ordered that we noticed Romeo Periera's wife was not with us. "Romeo you left your wife home?" "She's getting her daily fix," he replied. "What is that?" asked another. "It's called the Young and the Restless."

The focus next turned to Joseph Viera who was sitting next to me. He had been quiet the whole time taking in our comments. Joe Viera came to St. Stanislaus after spending some months at Mt. St. Benedict boys school in Trinidad from which he was expelled. The only thing I truly remembered about him was that he was always around, and that he was from a very wealthy family. Because he was always so disengaged from anything I cared about we seldom spoke. Despite that I would go up to him at midday after lunch and ask him to buy me a shaved ice. He would often do so, as he did for many others. Sometimes if I pushed my luck and asked too often he would say, "No, no not today I bought for you yesterday." He was never mean, condescending or judgemental. He was a nice guy but he did not care about school. Whether it was a funk that he had lapsed into when he was sent away and never got out of, or a learning disability, he never seemed to care. What he was clearly remembered for was his histrionics. He was thrown out of St. Stanislaus a number of times only to re-appear shortly afterwards. One event in particular made us all laugh. After committing a serious infraction, Joe was suspended by Father Hopkinson, the principal. "You can't suspend me," Joe remarked as he departed. That evening his father called the principal and convinced him to allow Joe to return the very next day; presto, the very next day the school had a brand new mechanical lawn mower. Even Joe who still remains passive in his demeanour, managed to smile at times as the stories about him were retold. Joe's real passions were to be found on the week-ends: fishing, hunting and camping.

By the time we began eating our lunch of BBQ chicken with rice, and macaroni and cheese we were all hungry. As usual Aubrey Kellawan with his long flowing hair was the first to try to belly up to the table, but Cyril DaSilva and Peter St. Aubyn seemed to be just waiting to give it to him. As soon as he had his plate in his hand, Cyril DeSilva said, "Aren't you going to let the women eat first?" It is customary to have the ladies eat first you know," chimed in St. Aubyn. "Let your wife eat before you," he said with a smile hoping to embarrass him. Aubrey Kellawan however was not deterred. He smiled broadly saying, "You guys think you are going to get me to leave this line. This is "first-come-first-served". Now you let your wives eat first." A few minutes later the three friends and drinking buddies were sitting next to each other eating and chatting. As we ate one could see the number of kites bobbing in the sky was increasing by the minute. The field next door was by then nearly filled with people raising kites or with kites in the air. Down the sea-wall in the distance the numbers were steadily increasing also.

Suddenly, an SUV appeared at the gate and made its way slowly towards our tent. "This is Billy coming with his wife at the wheel," said Carpy. He rose and walked out to greet them. Bobby and Billy Fernandes, the last of John Fernandes' 14 children, were twins and both were in our class. John Fernandes was a well-known businessman prominent in the Catholic Church. Carpy had told us beforehand that they both had Parkinson's disease. In addition, Bobby had a stroke and Bill was suffering from dementia. While Joe Viera would happily tell a master or the prefect that they could not throw him out because his father owned the school, Bobby and Billy acted as though their father had little or no influence at all. They were all-around nice guys with no airs or pretences and were friendly with everyone. Bobby was more the extrovert, the sportsman Billy more reserved. As the SUV came to a halt, Carpy opened the door and reached around to release Billy's seatbelt and help him out of the car. Billy's wife was out of the car in a flash standing next to him even though he needed no assistance. There was a hush in our tent as all eyes were then trained on his entrance. As he walked towards us we could all see Billy's condition for ourselves. He was slim and balding, but his drawn facial expression told the story of his illness, the way he held his hands and his shoulders drooped. It was clear some of his motor skills had been eroded. Carpy was serious and pale faced as he walked with him, while Billy's wife, an attractive and agile woman was smiling. She remained next to his side until he was well into the tent, and then left him in Carpy's care dashing over to greet Mrs. Carpenter and the other ladies. Billy came over and shook each of our hands like a politician working a crowd. As he did so his eyes focused on each of our faces. After making the rounds, Billy stood in front of the tent facing all of us. He waited for a few seconds and then began to speak. Everyone gave him full attention as he did so. He said he was glad for the love everyone had shown him, that he valued his friends, and that no amount of money could replace the love and friendship of his many friends and that of his wife. Halfway through his speech his words became inaudible, his mouth was moving but no sound was coming out. No one attempted to interrupt him. We were all transfixed by his demeanour. As he reached the end of what he was attempting to say, tears began to roll down his cheeks. Dale Morgan jumped up immediately and embraced him, as he fell slightly forward onto his shoulders. The rest of us sat there frozen, not knowing how to respond. Again his wife had rushed over to his side in seconds to comfort him. They both turned and walked towards their SUV. In leaving Billy looked older than when he walked in. His head bowed and he leaned forward, his shoulders slumped. She strapped him in, and was so gentle as she did so, patting him on his shoulders as though to reassure him. How fortunate he was to have such a woman by his side! She smiled and waved as she got behind the wheel. We were told they had to go to the hospital.

No one spoke until the SUV was well away. The departing car left one passenger who had come with them behind. Randy Bradford, Billy's brother-in-law had come with them to our picnic. Dale Morgan's first word to me once the silence was broken was, "Here comes Braddy again." The day before, when we had all met for the first time, Randy Bradford said to his old classmate Dale Morgan, "I heard that you are a professor at MIT now." Once Dale confirmed his statement Randy Bradford, rather than congratulate him exclaimed, "But you were in the B form." He seemed to be surprised that someone could transform themselves by dint of hard work and determination and reach the level of success Dale had. Dale delighted in repeating the story of their encounter especially since his son Colin was within earshot of them. I could also see he revelled in the attention given to his accomplishments. So it was interesting to see Dale purposely work his way towards where Randy Bradford was pontificating. True to form Braddy could not contain himself. He broke off his conversation and once again blurted out for all gathered to hear, "How come you are teaching at MIT? I don't remember you being an A student. You must have been a late bloomer." Dale threw his shoulders back and smiled broadly, his left hand cupping his cheeks with his index finger over his mouth as though to contain the laughter he had within. Some of the people gathered around, had no idea what was going on, or could not care; others were politely amused. Forty seven years after leaving St. Stanislaus, Braddy was still concerned about who the top dog was. It was not as if Randy Bradford himself had been a slacker. He had attended the University of Kansas on a scholarship and pursued a master's degree in Mathematics. He taught at the local university for a while and then did well as a manager in a technology firm in Canada.

About forty-five minutes after its departure Billy's SUV returned once more and we all got up to greet him. He seemed a lot more composed than when he came in the first time. Again he went up to each of his friends shook their hands and whispered something. When he came up to me he said, "I remember you. You used to work for Burnham." It was such a poignant detail that I smiled and cradled his extended hand with both of mine. After greeting us Billy grabbed some lunch and joined our conversation.

By this time the sun had begun to set and the skies were filled with a blaze of kites for as far as we could see. A cool breeze was blowing off the ocean once again. Colin Morgan, who had assured me several times he was enjoying the reunion, was standing several feet from the tent looking at the kites all around us. He seemed to be staring with deliberate focus at those towards Kitty. "Why do you think all of those kites are white?" he asked as I approached him. I was stumped for an answer. The kites in the field next to us all displayed a myriad of colours and all over the city we has seen colourful kites for sale. Why then were those in the sky in that one area all white? Dale emerged to investigate what we were curious about and he, too, was stumped but went on to suggest it was because of the clouds and the angle at which the kites were flying. With no better answer we left our questioning there. I returned to the tent and managed to have a little *tete-a-tete* with John Carpenter who was sitting alone sipping a bottle of water. I admired the discipline he showed in not having had a drink for the day. Just when it seemed the party would break up someone discovered that we did not eat a whole pot of cooked rice. Several of us got a second wind and charged over to the table. Once Dale Morgan heard "cook-up-rice" he raced over to the table extolling the goodness of this Guyanese specialty.

John Carpenter in his usual take charge manner arranged for each person who needed a ride to be taken home. Since the Headeckers had left a little earlier Bernard Friemann, Mark McWatt and I were left standing so eventually he arranged for Romeo Periera to drive us home. Pulling out in the car before us Colin Morgan pointed out that the clouds had lifted and the backs of the kites were showing their colours once again. Mark jumped into the front seat leaving Bunny and me to ride in the back and as we drove along our route back to our hotel, Romeo was pointing out who lived where, and offered a few comments about how they made their money. As we passed a massive five thousand square-foot house under construction he said, "I am not sure who is building that one, but if it is who I think it is, I think there might be some "white powder" on that one." We all broke out in laughter.

Once Romeo dropped us off at our hotel Mark, Bernard and I stood at the side of the road looking at the passing traffic. We were talking about the roads, the traffic flying past us and the size of the houses. Right across from where we stood was a case in point, a four thousand square-foot house painted light brown with red tiled roof festooned with tropical flowers. After lingering at the roadside chatting about the changes in the country, we continued for a while at the hotel bar where we drank coconut water.

GETTING OUT

The Easter holiday is a four-day weekend for most people in Guyana. Today was the first business day since I arrived so I made up my mind to set up a few appointments. I called the mayor's office, left a message, and went off to have breakfast. The Headeckers, Bernard Friemann and Mark McWatt were at breakfast when I arrived. Talk at the table centred around the events of the day before, kite flying, our picnic and the harrowing experience the Headeckers had trying to find a place to have dinner along Sheriff Street with its fast moving traffic and no sidewalks. I was just about finished breakfast when the mayor's office called. Mayor Hamilton Green told me he could meet with me either that day or the following so we arranged to meet at eleven thirty. He also mentioned he had to go to Parliament and might be able to get me in to listen to the budget debate going on at the time. I made a quick change from my shorts and casual shirt to a button down shirt and khaki slacks. I left in plenty of time so as to do some walking around before my appointment. The taxi dropped me off at the Georgetown Library where I planned to look at some newspapers. The lovely stone building had been well maintained and painted on the outside. Once inside I went upstairs where the attendants were all eager to help. The parquet floor had a few tiles missing in spots, not enough to make the place look shabby, but noticeable nonetheless, and the filing cabinets could not be closed because of the overflowing drawers. Downstairs, there were six to eight children playing in what seemed like a kindergarten class. In fact, they were children of staff members who did not want to leave them at home during the Easter school break. There were a number of people using the six computers downstairs, but the staff had no computers on their desks for their own use.

Once I finished my business at the library I walked down Avenue of the Republic and headed to City Hall. The sun overhead was bearing down on me and the humidity seemed to be increasing at every step. I mopped my forehead often with the paper towels I had in my pocket, hoping to stay dry and presentable for my appointment but I was fighting a losing battle. As I approached City Hall, I could see that the graceful building constructed in wood in 1889, and painted white with light blue trim, at first looked elegant in the mid-morning sun. Upon closer inspection, however, I saw that pieces of the structure were missing in different spots exposing wooden beams and showing a decay that, if not treated in time, could affect the building itself. As I walked into the compound I could see the building where the Constabulary was housed and it was in even worse shape than City Hall. The mayor's office, however, was in a secondary building and was in fine shape. As I entered I was directed to the second floor and emerged into a broad open space. Once I stated my business to the receptionist someone came to greet me. It was John Green, an assistant to the mayor. He ushered me into an inner office and I stood for a few seconds waiting while he went over and whispered to a person reading a document. I heard the distinctive voice of Hamilton Green ask a question and suddenly realized it was he who was sitting there in profile ten feet away. He rose to his feet, greeted me and ushered me into his personal office.

As soon as the pleasantries were out of the way the mayor began to elaborate on the woeful condition of the city and recited a persuasive litany of facts and figures to buttress his comments. He said the city did not collect any taxes from the many new buildings around and that was because valuation came under the Ministry of Finance which refused to act in the hope of cowing the City Council into adopting its own agenda. He spoke about the need to get a share of the "container tax" which trucks paid in compensation for their impact on city roads. He bemoaned the fact that "200,000 tons of garbage per day" were produced and the Council did not have enough trucks or a modernized means of disposal for that refuse. He confessed he had been mayor far too long, since 1996, and acknowledged the Peoples Progressive Party (PPP) was afraid to hold municipal elections for fear their party would not win. This resulted in their unpopularity in urban areas, and exposed them as the rural party they are. He said his plans for the revival of the city were all well worked out. The consultants he brought in had recommended there be no new construction of big buildings without the developer providing sufficient space for parking, something with which the Treasury initially agreed; but they later reneged on an agreement to implement the policy. Finally he cited the problems his own family was subjected to because the differences between him and the PPP government had become personal over the years. Somewhere in the middle of his explanation I began to lose interest in what the mayor was saying. It was like listening to one side of a bitter divorce battle that gave no consideration to its effect on the children!

At nearly eighty years of age, and sixty years in politics, Hamilton Green did not appear to be a man who was slowing down. Eighty pounds lighter than when we last spoke, he looked fit, and was anxious to show that there was some fight left in him by referring to himself as "Action Green" several times as he spoke. I concluded his explanation came from being asked the same questions about the city so often over the years. Just like in a bitter divorce, outsiders don't particularly care who is right when all can see that the children are being adversely affected. Differences between the national government, the PPP and the mayor of the most populous city in the country are nothing new in Guyana's politics. The same situation is being played out any day somewhere in the world. It is always sad when it happens, but is even more tragic when it happens in a country that can least afford such contentious infighting.

I left the mayor's office having fully made up my mind I was not going to call upon the other political leaders as I had planned. There was not much to understand.

Earlier that day, prior to my visit with the mayor, I noticed a woman with a big wad of cash counting money into the hands of two people standing next to her. I thought she was a money changer of some type. When I spotted her again later that day I wanted to see if my hunch was correct, so I approached her and asked to change twenty US dollars. At first she hesitated, appearing suspicious but I assured her I was not an official, just a tourist. Reassured, she changed my twenty at the going exchange rate.

I decided to visit my cousin Greta, the Registrar of births and deaths, since her office was nearby. I made my way in the blazing sun over to the General Post Office building. From the outside the building seemed to be as sturdy as when it was first built. Downstairs I was met with a sign I found surprising: "No three quarter pants, bi tights, no short skirts". The guard said it was the dress code for entering government offices. I found it odd there would be a dress code for people seeking to do business with the government. A dress code for the civil servants whom they employed was reasonable, but for the public? Luckily I did not have to worry.

The elevator in the building did not work and apparently had been out of order for some time so I had to walk up all four floors. As I made my way up the stairs I could see things go from bad to worse in front of my eyes. The metal window frames were rusted and frozen in the open position so that in a squall the rain blew in onto the stairs. The metal extension gates from the floor up were also rusted and frozen in place. Unlike City Hall, this was not a government office in any dispute with the central government and yet it was allowed to deteriorate, its moving parts becoming ossified. It seemed the government just did not care enough to spend money on facilities for the city. Since I did not tell my cousin what time I would arrive I thought I would take my turn in the line to see how things worked. As usual there were complaints galore by people who were waiting for long periods. Clearly there was some sort of system in place, for some people were tended to fairly quickly while others complained of having to return to the office several times. It is a common problem with government offices in most countries, but some are better than others. Most people seated in the hallway were well behaved despite having to wait so the police officers who acted as gate keepers did not have much to do. The officer tried to be helpful to some of those waiting and sympathized with others, but was careful not to get too involved. Interestingly, a number of people complained that more emphasis was put on enforcing the dress code set up for the public than in improving service to the people.

I went to the bathroom after sitting in the corridor for some time and I was surprised to find that there was no handle to flush. It was clear the whole building had not been upgraded since it was built in the early 1950's.

Once I decided I had waited long enough to see my cousin the Registrar, I asked the officer to see her secretary. She said my cousin had left for lunch, but she was scheduled to attend a meeting at another department straight afterwards and would not be back until much later. I left immediately after being given the news.

Downstairs, I desperately wanted to get a taxi to make my next appointment and avoid walking to the parliament building under the scorching sun but I was unsuccessful.

Reluctantly I began to walk. I was making my way there to listen in on budget hearings, accepting the invitation of Mayor Hamilton Green who said he also had to be there.

At Regent and Avenue of the Republic, I met a hawker selling, of all things, rat poison. He was standing in front of the table he had set up with about twenty small bags of rat poison. Next to him on both sides was a scale and he charged passers-by to weigh themselves. He did make a few sales of rat poison as I chatted with him but no one stopped to weigh themselves. A little further on just after I went by City Hall I came upon a man selling shaved ice. Both nostalgia and the need for something cool enveloped me at the same time. I bought one which was served to me in a plastic cup and I enjoyed my mid-afternoon treat while walking.

As I approached the Queen Victoria Law Courts I decided to stop in. I could see from a distance that the statue of the old Queen was back on her dais standing proudly for all to see. It was interesting to see her there even though the last time I saw her she was lying flat on her back at the rear of the Botanical Gardens. The wooden building opened in 1887 was constructed in the Tudor style, and was featured in tourism brochures as one of the interesting places to see in the city. The yard itself was well kept except for piles of cement left sitting around by those doing repairs. As I walked around I began looking for a waste basket to dispose of my empty shaved ice cup. I could not find a container for disposal and was determined not to throw it on the ground. Even upon entering the building I could not find a waste basket and, given how clean the inside of the building was, I could not bear to leave it in some corner. On the second floor I found five people in a seating area and asked where I could find a waste basket. Both the police guard and a person waiting suggested I put it on the floor in the corner. I refused. When they saw how adamant I was the people seated began to voice their opinion about the absence of waste baskets around the building and the city. Eventually the police guard relented, led me into a small office reserved for them a few feet away and said, "You could use this one." Inside I had a good look around a small courtroom in which a trial was about to begin. I would have liked to remain to see the judicial process at work but I had an appointment to keep so I left.

I finally arrived at the Parliament and as I entered the chamber the Mayor greeted me, gave me his seat and left. Just then the Minister of Housing rose to speak. Dressed in a dark suit and tie he gave a somewhat pedantic speech laced with figures to support his point of view. On two occasions he caused both the opposition and the gallery to erupt in uncontrolled laughter. The first was when he discussed the plans of the government to increase eco-tourism to the country. The opposition members hurled disparaging remarks at him pointing out that tourists could not be attracted to a garbage strewn city. Despite the heckling he pressed on, but when he referred to Georgetown as the "garden city" a louder laughter erupted. At another point in his speech he referred to the fine drinking water the city enjoyed. Again he was greeted by laughter and derision from the opposition. The Minister spoke for nearly forty minutes before taking his seat. I then listened to two short speeches by opposition members, and left when the chamber took a recess. I felt tired as I left the building, but I opted not to return to the hotel and instead to make the most of being downtown.

The sun had gone down by then, and the heat had given way to a cool light breeze. I headed out and walked over to the main fire station next door to Stabroek Market. Next door to that is the police station. I had to ask two ladies looking through the window whether the place was still in use. The stone structure had not been painted in some time and the wood around several of the windows was rotten, the frames sagging or absent. It was depressing just to step inside. I could not help wondering why so many government-owned buildings were in such a state of disrepair. They are clearly a blight on the area. Stabroek Market was about to close as I arrived but I was able to make the rounds to several stalls just for a look-see. Once I left the market, I made my way around the side which led to the wharf. It was an area I knew well at one time. As a child I would often have to go down to the wharf on Wednesday afternoons to collect a box of provisions sent by my parents from the Essequibo where they lived. There along the wharf would be boats bobbing up and down in the Demerara River. The sloops, all from different areas of the country, would come to deliver their produce to middle men who in turn supplied hucksters in the local markets. I wanted to see how things had changed and to relive my teenage years. As soon as I turned onto the driveway leading down to the wharf I could see the changes. The path was a hive of activity, lined with stalls selling all sorts of fruits and vegetables. Many of those buying seemed to be women making their way home after work and many of their bags had just a few items in them. It was difficult navigating my way down what was once the only cobbled path left in the city. When I reached the end I had to pass through a number of closed stalls and several times I had to skip over openings in rotten planks. At the end of the wharf, to my surprise, there were no sloops. I was told by one man that provisions came into the city by truck now or by smaller boats. "It is more direct," he said. On the other side of the stelling were a number of small ferry boats bobbing in the water. One captain informed me they ran to Vneed-en-Hoop. He said their service gave people two ways of getting into the city, by jitney or by boat. "Boat is better; it leaves you right in town." The tide was coming in as I stood there and the muddy water of the Demerara River was running strong. I stood for a minute to absorb the scene, to relive my teenage memories.

On my way out I met a gentleman who had nothing at all for sale in his stall. The five feet by six feet stall had a TV and a fan both of which were on. The man told me he and his two sons pretty much lived in the small space. He slept on the counter and his sons slept on the floor. At one point he had his three daughters with him also but Child Services had taken them away some time earlier. He and his children used the stand pipe further in the corner to shower, and could only do so late at night or early in the morning so as to avoid the authorities. Speaking to him gave me a window into a side of life I had seldom encountered. I wanted to get out of there before it got too late and became unsafe for someone who looked out of place. Just as I was about to leave, a burly half-naked man came down the aisle. "Where do you live?" I asked. "I sleep up there." "You mean you sleep on top of the stall," I said in disbelief. "Yes, me and many others." Neither he, nor the other man seemed ill fed or shabbily dressed; they simply could not afford lodgings in a city that no longer built affordable housing for low income workers.

Once I emerged from Stabroek Market wharf, I thought I might visit the DIH complex, a venue for liquor and beverage sales. I went upstairs to the rum shop. The place was pretty much the same as I recalled with a few modern touches. It was always a place for people who were waiting to catch the ferry, and where out-of-towners and hard drinkers went to imbibe. The big snooker table was replaced by something smaller and more current, and there were TV screens over the bar area. Even though it was clearly upgraded it was still fundamentally just a big rum shop. Next door, separated by palms and other potted plants, there was a newly added outdoor bar and deck which seemed to have the same clientele. At first when I entered the complex I thought I might get a drink, but the whole place had such a lack of character I left without doing so.

There were no taxis to be had around the area at that time of the early evening so I walked along Avenue of the Republic towards Regent Street where I thought I could get one easily. Just before I reached Regent Street, I came upon thousands of people milling around. At first I could not be sure what exactly they were all doing, crowded in such numbers like people waiting outside a venue for a rock concert or sporting event.

"What are all of these people doing here?" I asked someone at random. "Where do you want to go?" he asked in return. "We go to Mahica," he continued. Just then I saw the name Mahica written boldly on the back of the vehicle nearby and I realized I was in the midst of a depot of some sort. "What are all of these people doing in the city so late?" I asked myself. These could not all be government office workers or clerks in business offices. I was stumped for an answer to my question.

Since I was in the area I thought I might see what George Street looked like. It was the street on which the King George Hotel once was, a hotel my parents and I stayed in when we visited the city. All of the streets around that area were teeming with people walking back and forth, presumably to the next staging area of Stabroek Market a few blocks away. By then dusk had given way to dark. The street lights were on and it was then night. Suddenly, I heard someone call out in my direction, "You aren't supposed to be here." A man walked over to me and said, "You are not supposed to be in this area at this time. It's not safe here." "I am a Guyanese," I explained but then added "although I have not lived here for some time." "There are a lot of robberies and sometimes shootings around here. It's not safe," he said emphatically. "I could tell you are a stranger." I kept wondering how he knew I was a stranger?" After all, I had no camera and carried nothing that would reveal me as a foreigner; or could it be that I was looking up and around too often. I looked at him, he was a tall stout man dressed in long pants and a short sleeve shirt. I was a little puzzled that he could pick me out as being out of place though the only difference in our dress was that I wore a long sleeved shirt. Then he directed me, "Walk with me to the open well-lit street then get a taxi." I did not feel as afraid as he was for me, but I accompanied him and got a taxi. That was what I was in the process of doing anyway. I thought it was an interesting encounter.

Back at the hotel, the Headeckers, Bernard Friemann and Mark McWatt were all sitting around a large table discussing their first visit to the city. No one was upset or angry about what they saw, but they were quite disappointed. Brian Fung relayed his having to point out to his sister Bonnie where their house once stood, and the funeral parlour nearby. He went on to recall the way some people behaved when they attended funerals, fortifying themselves with alcohol before going into the funeral parlour. Bonnie for her part remembered very little about Georgetown, and explained her lack of memory and nostalgia by her sheltered upbringing. She related where they were allowed to go and where they were not. Peter Headecker said he was disappointed his house was no longer there, and he had trouble recognizing the place where it once stood. He was particularly disappointed he was denied entrance to our old school, St. Stanislaus, because he and the men in the group were wearing shorts. Their disappointment was overcome when they visited the Catholic Cathedral further down the road on Brickdam. They all praised the way it had been maintained and urged me to include it on my agenda. He said that worst place of all was the Georgetown Zoo and the Botanical Gardens. He deplored the conditions in which the animals were kept and noted that the flowers had not fared much better. Then he spoke about the garbage around the city. There was a consensus that it alone made them even more depressed than they otherwise might have been. It was distraction that made us view everything we saw through that prism.

HOUSEKEEPING

My own lack of forward planning meant I was unable to make the trip to Kaieteur Falls. Everyone who wanted to go did so long before we arrived but I planned instead to visit relatives that day. When I arrived downstairs for breakfast I was surprised to see everyone still eating because I thought they would have been long gone by then. At the table Peter Headecker was telling Mark McWatt and Bunny Friemann about the experience he had the night before at a dinner party given for them by Bonnie's uncle. He raved about the dinner itself, and had high praise for Bonnie's aunt who had prepared the meal. What irritated him, however, was the attitude of one guest in particular who extolled the progress the country had made, and who went on to say that there was no country like his own that could provide the lifestyle he had. I gathered the conversation around the table was pretty heated and involved many others when Peter said, "I don't know where these people get all this self-confidence from."

I reminded him that many people who hailed from Guyana have always spoken that way. It's just that those of us who have lived in North America for so many years have forgotten that. I told him I, too, had noticed an over-confidence in the future speaking to people from taxi drivers to professionals. What I did not think of saying as we spoke was that our reaction might be a reflection of our age and an attempt to justify the decisions we made in our youth. I remember distinctly the aspirations my own friends and I had when we were in graduate school. It was certainly not to emigrate. Quite often, when Commonwealth students would gather in an impromptu setting we would speculate that the time would come when we could work for an American or international corporation while living in our own country. That dream had taken much longer than many of us thought it would, but it had happened for a few of our friends from India. It was also a dream that had come true for some people like our friend John Carpenter and others who, though living Guyana, travelled to North America regularly to see friends, doctors etcetera. Indeed, just before leaving the US I told my son David about Carpy and he said to me, "You guys were afraid to take a chance." That hurt, but he was right. The more immediate reasons for the self-confidence of the people we met might have surrounded us as we spoke. In front of us was a bar stocked with wines from the US, Europe and South America. Alongside the bar were TV sets tuned to programming from many of those same regions. Across the street stood houses, exact models of which could be found in Florida or Arizona. What then did they lack? The debate turned on the question of quality and preference.

The minibus to pick the group up eventually arrived, and they departed for Kaieteur Falls. I caught a taxi into Georgetown to meet my brother Arthur.

We walked to the Bank of Nova Scotia to meet my friend Horace Nurse, from whom I had asked to borrow money. The bank itself had a line some fifty people long. I wondered what so many people were doing in this particular bank especially since there were so many banks around. When we got to the front of the line we found out I could easily access my own account in the US so I did not need Horace after all. Horace insisted we go to New Thriving for lunch. Once lunch was over Arthur and I hopped into a taxi and went to La Repentir Cemetery to visit my father's grave. The road into the cemetery gave the suspensions of the taxi a good work out. The whole place was overgrown in every direction. I could not believe the height of the grass and the size of some of the trees. Arthur knew the exact location of the grave, as both he and my brother Noel visiting from the US had cleaned up the area a short time earlier. The tomb next to my father's was in particularly good shape. The area around was clear of all weeds and the headstone was painted a light blue. My dad's and the one on the opposite side showed signs of cracking and its paint had faded. As we were about to depart we were approached by two young men. One was on a bicycle and the other, with a cutlass in his hand, was on foot. They introduced themselves to us and gave me their card. Their business was to upkeep the grave sites of families who engaged them to do so. "What a business I thought!" I stayed there with my brother for half an hour or so then we departed.

Just when I began to wonder if we would have to walk all the way out of what some said could be a dangerous place our taxi re-appeared. The driver thought we might need him so he had stayed around. I directed him to take us to my cousin Esme's home in the Ruimvelt Housing complex. We had a little trouble finding the place but eventually arrived. She lived in a very small house not much different from the original ones built for low income workers in the late 1950's. As I looked around before entering the yard I could see the changes made by other families to their original properties. Many were rebuilt in concrete as modern dwellings double the size with verandas reflecting a more middle class preference and sensibility. These were the third and fourth generations to live in these houses so it was interesting to see the changes.

When I went to visit Aunt Olga she gave me the telephone numbers of many family members I had hoped to see. I called to say I would drop by at some time but I could not be more specific. Luckily Esme was home when Arthur and I got there. Esme is my Uncle Harold's daughter and was born and raised in Buxton. Her father was the only one of his siblings who stayed in their original village once they became adults. On several Sundays a year my father would take us by taxi to visit his brother. Just before I left Guyana Esme got a job in Georgetown. Several times a week she would come to our house to have lunch with us so we became great friends. Since my departure I knew very little about her life and had not seen her. I took a seat in her tiny sitting room and waited. Within a minute, she emerged and looked very much like the person I remembered. Her features had remained the same. She had no wrinkles and stood tall with the same bright smile. Her grey and black hair was pulled tightly back and she was a bit heavier. Time had clearly treated her well as it was hard to believe she was 73. We talked about her life since I last saw her, her marriage, the death of her husband thirty years earlier and about her brothers and sisters. We talked also about the serious arthritis that had affected her mobility. She said she always knew what was going on with me because Uncle Jack and his family, who lived a few blocks over, always shared with her the contents of the Christmas card I sent them. I was surprised and pleased at that and smiled broadly. It was heartening to know that, after not ever receiving any communications from Uncle Jack over so many years, he appreciated that I sent him a card and shared the contents of my note inside with other family members. We spent nearly an hour with Esme and then left. She wanted to call a taxi for us but we opted to walk and try for a taxi on our own because I wanted to see more of the area.

We walked out to the main road and then remembered that a good friend of mine, Gwendolyn Anthony, once lived somewhere nearby. We made a half-hearted attempt to find the house but quickly gave up since we were on foot. We were, however, able to find my Uncle Jack's house. I don't know why I so wanted to see my Uncle's house even though he and his wife had passed away. I just knew it was one of the places I always hoped I could find on my own whenever I thought of returning to Georgetown. He was one of those people I had hoped I would see upon my return but I was late by just a few years. Uncle Arnold (called Jack) had died at 96 years old, three years earlier, and his wife Aunt Elaine, had died months later at the age of 90. They were married to each other for 62 years and had seven children. The gate to their home was padlocked, and the neighbors informed me that my cousin who occupied the house with his son was at work. I looked around at the other homes, some rebuilt, and then left.

As we walked away who should we see coming down the road walking towards us? None other than cousin Aubrey who had visited me at my hotel a few days earlier. He gave us a big hug and invited us to come back to the house with him but we declined. We spoke for a minute or so then we both went on our way. Long after I had left Guyana and after I began writing about my trip, a memory suddenly flashed into my mind. I had always remembered going to Georgetown for a vacation with my parents from where we lived on the Essequibo coast. We went to visit Uncle Jack and Aunt Elaine who at that time lived in a ranch house near Camp and Lamaha Street. Seeing so many families living in one house, washing their dishes and housewares at a common pipe in the yard and sharing a common bathroom, had made an impression on me as a young boy of nine. What I had forgotten was that months later a letter arrived for my father from Uncle Jack. The discussion I overheard between my parents was about his request that my father write a letter of recommendation for him to get a house in a new development, and affirm that he would stand as guarantor for this undertaking. My father was so concerned to make sure the forms were filled out correctly, and the letter of recommendation well-written that he gave it to my mother to vet. It was not a big deal in our house but to Uncle Jack it must have meant the world. I doubt whether anyone in our family would remember the incident because it was never mentioned again and even I don't know why I remembered it so vividly. All I remember of my uncle was that he was an affable man whose determined focus was on one thing - his family.

We left my cousin Aubrey standing in the street a few yards away from his home and walked a few blocks where we caught a taxi. All day long I had been carrying around a number of chocolate bars I wanted to give to Aunt Olga. I had brought the chocolates at the request of my friend Horace who acquired a taste for them when he visited me and fell in love with the particular brand sold near my house in Riverside, Connecticut. Because of his request I thought she might like some also. It had been a task all day to keep them from melting in the hot sun as we went from place to place.

The car dropped us at Aunt Olga's house. She was at home alone and came down to greet us. She was glad to see me once again and reminded me that I had pledged to visit her at least three times before I left. I told her of my activities on that day and she was especially glad to hear I did not forget my father and my cousins. "You know Reynold we are not a close family. We are not in and out of each other's business, but we have always loved each other and stayed in touch with each other. I'm glad you went to see Esme," she said as we departed.

It was late afternoon by then so my brother Arthur, who had been with me all day, and I walked down Albert Street looking for a restaurant. We went into what seemed like a popular place. Inside it was a tad dark, but it was clean and organized. It was clearly a neighbourhood hangout. I ordered some "cook-up-rice" and some chicken. The meal did not disappoint so I was delighted with my choice. While eating I saw a woman with red hair looking down from a little office on the side of the kitchen. I was told she was the owner and had been running the establishment for more than five years. I was not surprised because the one thing noticeable throughout the city was how many of the businesses were owned and run by women. Satisfied with my meal I bid my brother goodbye and we each got into a taxi going in different directions.

Back at the hotel, I was astonished to see that the whole party was relaxing at a table in the air-conditioned dining room. I thought perhaps they did not go to Kaieteur but, much to my surprise, they explained they did indeed go and had a great time. It dawned on me what a small country Guyana really is contrary to what most Guyanese think. As I sat down to join the group Mark McWatt said Bonnie Headecker had insisted on saving me a few of the crab backs and some black pudding that her uncle's family had brought for them. As he was speaking Bonnie had already moved from her seat next to Peter and was on her way over to me with a plate. The crab backs and black pudding were delicious. I had forgotten about crab backs until Peter Headecker mentioned he had them the evening before at their dinner. I have never seen them anywhere in my travels and had not thought about them in years. On the other hand, I had discovered much to my surprise that many people the world over make blood pudding. You could imagine my surprise when I ate blood pudding in an upscale restaurant after being told for years that it was what slaves ate. From the conversation at the table I gathered everyone had a good time on the trip to Kaieteur. Bunny Friemann was intrigued by the large clearings for newly established small towns used as bases for gold mining in the bush and said they flew over many of them.

ROAD TO BOUNTY

There was no time for breakfast or even coffee. The minibus Peter and Bonnie Headecker ordered arrived early to take us to the Georgetown Club. Rather than have it wait around we all got aboard and took off some fifteen minutes early. We zipped into Georgetown in very light traffic and when we arrived at the Georgetown Club John Carpenter and his wife were already there waiting for us, along with Peter St. Aubyn and his wife. John's car was loaded with stuff for our picnic and he greeted us as we emerged from the minibus. "Good you are all here. Now let me see where the larger bus is." He got on his phone while directing us to make ourselves comfortable on the chairs scattered around. But I could not sit. I realized I was in a place few local people in my youth ever got to visit. At that time the Club was a place to socialize for the elite managers of the sugar estates, the managers of foreign owned enterprises and the professionals who serviced them. It was mainly an all-British affair and exclusively an all-white affair. What hit me as I stood to the side looking around the ground floor was how sparse the place was. It looked deserted. What was I hoping to see here? It was always just a building. It was the people who gathered here who made the place so special and they were long gone. It was one of the misfortunes of the Colonial era that countries like Guyana, which had some of the best managed sugar estates in the world brought in foreign specialists to operate them, people who had no intention of remaining after their service was over. Consequently the country did not have access to their expertise after they returned to their British employers. They all decamped *en masse* to Australia, Canada or New Zealand

John Carpenter was on the phone speaking to the bus operator advising him that we were ready to get on our way and the bright red bus with the logo "The Night Rider Bus Service" arrived shortly thereafter. We piled onto the bus as John Carpenter and a few others loaded some items. Again Carpy was on the phone checking with our hosts at Bounty Farms to make sure all the necessary preparations were made. Every time I met John Carpenter, Romeo Periera and their wives it was interesting to see how punctual they all were. Once we began driving through the city on the way to Bounty Farms, John Carpenter began to point out different landmarks giving a commentary about them. When we reached the area called Houston, the bus pulled aside and picked up Joe Viera's wife, Paula and her sister and, further up, we stopped to pick up Victor Yhap and his wife also. There was the usual reminiscing for short periods, the most amusing of which was recalled by Peter St. Aubyn. He told us that one day a policeman pulled John Carpenter aside for speeding. "Are you aware you were going over the speed limit sir?" said the policeman. "No sir that could not be so. I was watching myself carefully." "Well the speed gun says that you were." "I think your speed gun is wrong. I think it needs to be fixed. Here's the money for you to get it fixed." He was then allowed to drive on.

By this time on our trip I had begun to digest what I had seen so far and reached some conclusions. I decided I absolutely liked the changes I had seen. The old wooden buildings we lived in were in most instances too small. Most of the kitchens could not accommodate the modern conveniences of today; they were just too small. Even the height of the new houses did not bother me as much anymore because I realized there was nowhere else to go but up given the constraints of the lot sizes. That is something we Americans are well aware of as are people in many other big cities of the world. The sight of "McMansions" in our midst has been a fact of constant debate over the years. For us, travelling back to the Guyana of our youth forced us to confront these new realities in a few days. Even those Guyanese residents who disliked the new look of the city objected not to the changes themselves but to the architectural detail of the new buildings.

We reached Bounty Farms after an uneventful ride up the East Bank Highway. The bus was unusually quiet on the way up. I guess most of us were just preoccupied, absorbing the new scenery. A large gate swung open to let us into the farm, and the driver was directed by both the gateman and Carpy to go down to the end of the road. As we proceeded, we passed a large painted concrete structure on our right and a large chicken pen on our left. As the bus crawled in further we passed some orange trees in a field with a number of sheep grazing under them. The small trench that ran the length of the farm was weeded and the water was flowing out as we entered. At the end of the road was a large cabana with a thatched roof. A swimming pool in front of the cabana was fed by water from a nearby creek. The water in the pool was dark like a rich coffee. Shielded as it was from prying eyes by a fence with tropical plants around it made the sight a very inviting one. We took our seats under the gazebo, and looked around in awe at the well-manicured sections of the property, but more especially at the well placed tropical plants that adorned the landscape. Nearly everyone who had not been there before had something to say about the landscape or the plants. Aubrey Kellawan was the first to rise from his seat, his pronounced long hair flapping around his shoulders as he said, "I am going for a walk," and with that he took off. A number of people followed him in quick succession. I, too, was eager to see the back of the property so I followed on my own. The area in the rear was formed by the beautifully manicured area between it and the cabana. In one area of the expanse there was an island in the middle of a pond and a small boat with a paddle to row out to it. The second pond was approximately the same size and configuration but had a narrow walking path to get to it. The setting gave me a sense of calm, a sense of tranquillity as I traversed the area. With a view of so many flowers and tropical plants in the area, one could not help but feel a sense of peace. It was exactly the kind of setting that helped some of us rekindle the memory of our youth. As I approached the rear of the property my feet sank and the earth moved as though I were on a small boat on heavy seas. I recognized where I was immediately. I was standing on a patch of pegasse, a loose bog-like land formation that is largely unfit for agriculture. It is a feature that makes sizable portions of land unusable in Guyana.

Back at the cabana John Carpenter had the BBQ going. With the sun and the humidity much stronger by then he looked quite the part of a pit master, greying hair prominently displayed in the bright sunshine and his rugged face contorted as he tried to control the hot fire. Toward the entrance of the cabana a few people had gathered around a man whose arms kept motioning as he spoke to them. "That is David Fernandes, Bobby and Billy's nephew. He is the manager of the farm," John Carpenter answered. "Go over and talk to him. He is a nice guy. These are all his plants; he put them here."

David Fernandes is a six foot tall strapping fellow with aviator glasses, an agile look and a broad smile. He liked the compliments my friends were heaping on him about the farm and his face lit up even more when they asked about the different plants around. What impressed me most initially as I joined the conversation was that he knew the botanical name of each plant and where they came from. When my friends complimented him he repeated twice, "The farm was Uncle Billy's idea. I only added to it." When I became more direct in questioning him he admitted plants were a passion of his, a "hobby" he had acquired over the years. I commented about the many varieties of croton plants he had on the property, and asked him about the varieties of orchids. He must have realized I had more than a passing interest in flora because he said quite suddenly, "Do you want to see my collection? If you have fifteen minutes I can show you." With that we headed for his pick-up truck parked nearby. As we drove slowly off the property he gave a few orders to workers through the window. Then he told one person he was heading home for a few minutes. In talking while we drove he stressed once again that the farm was his Uncle Billy's idea, that he had taken it to another level but that Uncle Billy had started it. He said that in order to make his vision for the farm come through he had to undergo a process. "This is a family business, it's a team effort, so I had to submit my proposal to our Board. I asked for a certain amount of money and to their credit they backed me. They thought my estimate for the project was too low so they gave me more money than I asked for. But it was up to me to make it work." It was hard work, and it took some time but he was given time and space to carry out his vision. As he spoke I could see the pride he took in his successful achievement. Everything about his demeanour and his speech conveyed quiet self-confidence. He had gone to school locally but was quick to add that, going forward, the farm would be in good hands because his cousin was at school in the US and would be back to join him. His house, less than a quarter mile away, was tucked away from the highway by trees. The first thing I noticed once we turned into the yard was the number of birds around. He said he had two bird feeders on both sides at the rear of the house that attracted a number of humming birds and several other species as well. He dropped me off in front of his house where he had many potted plants in an early stage of growth. They were all displayed in such a way that one would suspect a professional botanist had been involved. On his property he had a number of attractive palm trees including a fan palm and a high eucalyptus tree. One palm tree in particular stood out, a high Bismark palm which David said was from Southeast Asia.

I was so engaged in looking at his saplings and other plants that it took me a few minutes to realize I was in another section of Bounty Farms. Next to his house were two giant hatcheries and opposite was a large chicken coop with a number of birds. It was wonderful to see how efficient, clean and well managed the place was. David Fernandes was the third generation of a family business that was a little-advertised success story of Guyana.

As we travelled back to the main farm in his pick-up truck David filled me in on the way the farm was set up to produce 120,000 chickens a week. When I suggested his plants would do wonders to improve the look of the city of Georgetown, he told me he met a minister of the government and made that suggestion to him, but the offer was never taken up. I wanted to tell him he should take another stab at it because educating politicians on the need for such an undertaking is generally a slow and agonizing process.

Back at our gathering under the cabana things were in full swing. Just after I returned Lennox Benjamin, Benj, as they called him, arrived. He looked as he did in school, the same forward leaning posture, the same gait and hair style. He was a little heavier now but flashed the same quick smile as he met his fellow classmates. He apologized for not coming to our earlier get-together but said that as chief statistician for the government he needed to be present for the budget debates.

Lunch was about to be served since John Carpenter's Barbecue was nearly done. Carpy's wife Colleen insisted that we classmates take a picture before we ate. Once the photos were taken, and just as we began to eat both Bobby and Billy

Fernandes arrived to join us. We had seen Billy earlier so all eyes were on Bobby as they approached us up the walkway. We knew that Bobby, like Billy, had Parkinson's but we were aware that he had also suffered a stroke and it was apparent that it had a slight effect on his physiognomy as well as his gait. Everyone was glad to see both brothers and rose to greet them. After lunch people drifted off into little groups to chat. Dale Morgan and his son Colin were still on a high about the family dinners they were being invited to, and Bunny Friemann just seemed to be floating on air as he moved from one group to the other. Everyone was basking in the glow of being with people with whom they had a visceral connection, an unspoken bond for which there were no words necessary.

John Carpenter once again reiterated his speech about the philanthropic aspect of our reunion. He sang the praises of the student we had sponsored so far, and again raised the question of whether we would like to sponsor her through to her Masters degree or stop at her first degree as was our original intention. He reminded us to make our contributions in a timely manner and urged us to think about where we would like to meet next in two years. He suggested we could meet again in Guyana, or on a Caribbean island or somewhere else. He ended by saying he planned to invite our student to the Georgetown Club on Saturday so we could meet her. It was interesting to see how dedicated Carpy was about this philanthropy because he had raised it at every gathering since we arrived.

Just as many of us were beginning to fade someone suggested we have the poetry readings. Cyril Da Silva proposed that we have an emcee, and Peter St. Aubyn urged Randy Bradford to be it. With a little prodding Bradford stepped into the role like a pro. He walked to the front of gathering and promptly determined the order in which readers would go. He began by begging our indulgence for a few seconds and introduced the son of his friend Colin Morgan. He said he had already told his daughter about Colin because, if Colin were anything like his father, he would be very good at what he did. He noted that Colin's father Dale was in the "B Form" and had risen to become a professor of physics at MIT, although he admitted he was baffled by Dale's transformation! Some people were confused about what Braddy meant by this introduction and others, who knew them both just smiled.

It was an odd spotlight into which Colin Morgan had to step. He recited three poems and, upon request, did a fourth. We could see he had some talent and he was given an ovation. Without much fanfare Braddy then called on Robert (Bobby) Fernandes. Even though he had come unprepared, Bobby went on to recite two poems. He, too, was given a standing ovation. We were all glad to see that his illness had not degraded his mental ability and zest for living. Randy Bradford then with great fanfare introduced Mark McWatt, the award winning poet. Mark rose from his seat, walked to a spot from which all could see him, texts in hand, and with panache delivered five poems. He told a poignant story to set up each piece so as to give context to his words and to pique our interest. It was a pleasure to listen to him and see his polished performance. He was urged by the gathering to do one last piece and he obliged us by doing one of his more earthy efforts. Everyone loved it. It was a compelling note on which to end, so noteworthy that it caused Peter St. Aubyn to exclaim, "See! That's what I call a poem, it has women and it has liquor."

Despite the inviting swimming pool at our disposal only Brian Fung and Victor Yhap ventured in. I suppose the rest of us were too self-conscious. We hung around until late afternoon when a number of people began to clean up. Most of us joined in and with large sturdy garbage pails all around the cabana it was a painless exercise. We departed around 6:00 pm for Georgetown. On our way back Bonnie Headecker was on the phone trying to arrange for our minibus to pick us up as scheduled. Despite her best efforts she could not reach the driver to let him know we were *en route*. The recording on the number he gave her indicated that no person by that name was around. We were frustrated once we reached Georgetown with no transportation to take us to our hotel but, once again, Carpy swung into action. He made a few calls and then announced that the bus we had arrived in, which was at that moment starting to pull away, would instead be made available to take us to our hotel.

Once in my room I found two messages waiting for me; one from my brother Arthur, and another from my old friend David De Groot. I was super-excited to finally get a message from my good friends David and Cheryl De Groot for I had asked every friend or acquaintance since I arrived for their number or address. I called the number immediately and got Cheryl on the telephone. She sounded like the same vivacious person I once knew. She insisted we meet as soon as possible so we arranged to have lunch the following day, scheduling time and place early the next morning.

YOU NEVER WROTE

When I arrived downstairs for breakfast in the hotel dining room there were only two people there, Bonnie (Fung) Headecker sat chatting intimately with her brother Brian. They were so engrossed in private conversation that it took them a few seconds to recognize another person had entered the room and walked over to the coffee station. Because they sat so close to each other and leaned in ear to ear I wondered whether I should join them. My apprehension was dispelled when Brian took notice of me and said, "Come over and join us." I soon got around to asking Bonnie about her feelings for Guyana after having spent a couple of days travelling around to see those places she once knew. She was still quite certain the trip was no more than a holiday to her, and she did not feel any intimate connection to the country. Strangely her brother Brian Fung felt a bit differently and Bonnie commented, "That's because you worked here and I didn't." We realized almost simultaneously that those of us who had worked in Guyana even for a short while, as her brother had done, had more of a connection to the place than those who did not. Part of my own disorientation was due to the great number and type of new dwellings erected during my absence, but my connection to family and friends somehow made me better able to digest the changes. I think my interest in Bonnie's reaction to her native country sprang from my own desire to compare the reaction of people like me who had not been in Guyana for a long time. We were not alone for very long before the rest of the party joined us for breakfast. Midway through our meal a person from the main office came over to tell me I had a call in the office. It was Cheryl De Groot. She explained she could not meet me for lunch as planned because something had come up. Instead, her husband David was on his way to meet me.

Back at the breakfast table the talk was about whether they would get the group to visit Guyana Distilleries and there was some confusion about the number of people who could go on the tour. We were debating the activities of the day when David De Groot appeared at the entrance to the restaurant and I jumped up to greet him. As he shook my hand and embraced me he said, "But you never wrote." It was a strange thing to say and, although true, it struck me like a knife. I was speechless for a few seconds and could think of no appropriate reply. I met his son and then rushed them over to meet my friends, David's words still ringing in my brain. David, a salesman by profession, asked each of them pointed questions about their family connection to the city and actually remembered the relatives of the Fung clan. Brian, who had emerged as the photographer in residence by then, made us pose for photographs. David's face had not changed noticeably though he was heavier and moved more slowly. He is just as intelligent and engaging and has retained the charm that has been part of his persona from his days as a salesman.

As we sat down at a separate table to have a private conversation he began by saying once again, "Man, you never wrote." Still lost for an answer I replied, "You look well." "I am 81 now, but I am getting along." I rushed to thank him for all the kindnesses he had extended to me when we worked in the same office and I recounted, partly for his and partly for his son's ear, the various meetings and assignments he had included me in even though I was never in his area of responsibility. He had seen me as an eager young person and was determined after a long memorable conversation to be my sponsor. I had enjoyed working with him and, at times, partying with him and his wife all over the city. I had to think hard to recall the many things we did so long ago so as to prolong speaking to him lest he use those dreaded words again. He told me about his wife Cheryl and her new health regimen, and of his change of political party. We chatted about his son and his business and some of the setbacks he had. It was obvious to me as we spoke that David wanted to accomplish more than he had. The big breaks simply never came his way despite his ability and charm. It occurred to me that he might have gotten his shot if only friends like me had returned.

We chatted for nearly ninety minutes before he had to leave. The one person who we remembered most was Frank Pilgrim. Although he was by then dead for two decades, he was such a good and dear friend to us both and so instrumental an advisor to both our careers that we could never forget his kindness. He was a true professional who began as a journalist at the local newspapers, before ending up at the guardian as their West African correspondent. We know him when he returned to become Public Relations Officer to the then Prime Minister. And, just like the big hearted person he always was, he offered to give me a ride into the city. I returned to my room put on my sneakers and got into his SUV. By that time it must have been in the high 80's and humid. We did not chat very much on the way, unlike in the old days when conversation between us flowed and we commented on everything.

I got off on the Avenue of the Republic, said farewell, and ran into the brutal mid-day sun. I headed straight for Hibiscus Lane where arts and crafts are sold. I looked around for a while and then went over to check out William Fogarty's, a once-venerable department store. I was disappointed with both the quality of products and the poor efforts to display them. It seemed clear that standards of presentation were all but abandoned by the constant exodus of people talent and know-how. Losing so many skilled people so quickly obviously had a severe impact on an already fragile economy. Under such circumstances people either succumb to their plight, sink into despair or soldier on as best they can.

I walked over to Guyana Stores, formerly Bookers Stores. The sun and humidity were fierce, even to walk over one block. There the story was the same. The goods were put out in a "take it or leave it" manner. The quality and range of products each store carried seemed to suggest this was no longer the main shopping area of the city, that things had become more widely dispersed with a number of specialty stores taking their place. It was sad to see that the old stores I knew had faded so badly.

Outside I was tempted to catch a taxi to my hotel because it was just too hot. But when I saw so many people going about their business I told myself, "If they can do it so can you. After all this is home." So I walked along Church Street to the office of my good friend Cynthia on Carmichael Street. She worked for an agency of the Ministry of Health and was situated in a well maintained building. Her air-conditioned office was modern, with a telephone and computer, and a few local handicrafts around. She explained their budget was fully funded because a particular minister had taken a personal interest in her area. We talked about some of my observations and impressions. When I mentioned the state of many of the buildings, particularly the government buildings, she asked if I had seen the Bishops High School. She said its pristine condition was due to the fact that her class was the first to begin raising money abroad for its upkeep and improvement when it became obvious the government was not doing so. Now, many years later students from other schools do the same in New York, London, Toronto, as they did. She was proud of the example her group had set and it was good to see a building that was not run-down, one which had all of the conveniences of a modern office.

I left and walked along Church Street to Austin Book Services. It was a well-stocked store with lots of books by Caribbean writers and also text books and novels from around the world. After I had my fill of browsing I made a small purchase and walked down Camp Street for a block or two. I gave up when I began thinking about how far I might have to go and instead took a taxi to my hotel. Before I left the United States I had planned to rent a moped or some such vehicle, but after seeing so many cars on the road and the speed at which they drove, I did not even bother to inquire.

Back at my hotel my friends were all having some refreshments. It turned out they never left for the Guyana Distilleries tour. There were problems with the time and numbers and, because it was a Friday, traffic was a problem. We were facing the ocean, however, and a gentle breeze came through every so often to temper the heat and humidity. After chatting for a long while we agreed on a time to meet for our evening engagement.

The party was at Joe Vieira's house and every one of us knew where it was. It was the only place Dale Morgan and I recognized on our way in from the airport. The Vieira compound, with its sumptuous modern houses set back from the main road, always attracted the eye as one passed by. Having disliked being in school as much as he did, Joe opted early for the family business of managing their sugar estates. In quick order he married and settled into a newly erected dwelling on the family compound. Our minibus, which had left us in the lurch a few nights earlier, arrived well before the designated time to pick us up. We boarded the bus and zipped up to the Houston area in short order. By this time both the heat and humidity had dropped substantially. It had become comfortable and the early evening air made the trip enjoyable. As we drove by I could see my friends still stared out of the windows wide eyed as we passed once familiar places. Paula, in a sleeveless party dress, came out to meet and welcome us. From the time we entered the gate we could see this was a carefully maintained residence, the property surrounded by tropical plants and flowers. We passed the section under the house used as a carport and emerged in the rear to a wide expanse of beautifully manicured lawn with a pool and bar. Joe sat on a chair next to the bar watching us approach. Many of us thanked him for having us over, which brought a smile to his face. Joe was pleasant throughout the evening but I wondered if he remembered any of us, even those who told stories about his legendary escapades at school. From where I stood I could see Paula welcoming her guests and directing the staff. When she eventually made her way to where we stood she seemed concerned that people were not drinking. As a matter of fact the barman commented to me before she arrived, "You guys don't seem like a drinking crowd." They were both right; we were an older crowd, accustomed to top end liquor, so there was little rush to imbibe. Paula went off and began arranging for food to be served. It was a well-organized and much appreciated party, but I felt there was something lacking. Not in the surroundings or anything like that, but in the event itself. We were all in different ways reliving the past with friends we might not meet again. There was an air of nostalgia.

The highlight of the party turned out to be when our dear classmate James Fitzpatrick turned up. He had remained in Guyana, in Bartica where he grew up. He was much slimmer than I remembered him in high school, and his distinctive honey coloured face did not show the signs of age. He had the same smile and readily shared the details of his life with us. He would not come into the party and mingle, preferring to sit on a chair positioned near the entrance at the front of the yard. Everyone offered to get him something to eat and drink, but our hostess had already taken care of that. It was good to see our friend, and to see that he was happy.

Surprisingly Colin Morgan seemed to be enjoying our party. He did not stray too far from his father's side and seemed to enjoy the incessant recounting of past experiences and seeing his father's joy at being among his boyhood friends. Dale Morgan summed up their feeling best when he observed, "There is something to be said for completion."

As the evening wore on something that had been percolating came to the fore. Some people wanted to go to "63 Beach" on the Corentyne, a known local hangout of our youth. I was having my dinner at a table near Colleen Carpenter when her husband John came and asked for our opinion about making an excursion there. If a sufficient number of people would like to go I could easily arrange for a bus to take us," John Carpenter insisted. I was surprised by the swift and emphatic reply of his wife, "The place is a dump!" To which the other wives nodded with approval. Then she went on in a rather loud voice looking straight at her husband, "Keep your old memories, the place is a dump." Carpy seemed jolted for a few seconds, but then he recovered and quite diplomatically said, "Well we will see what the consensus is." Sitting there, and seeing that brief exchange I knew that idea was a dead issue. Throughout the evening music from the 1960's and 70's played softly in the background. As we departed a little after eleven "Me and Mrs. Jones" filled the air.

ADJUSTING

Staying at a hotel just out of the city had its drawbacks. We were not able to step outside and walk around town. On the other hand we had plenty of time to share stories and views on nearly every subject. Shortly after we started breakfast Bonnie's uncle arrived. I gathered from a brief exchange between her and her husband Peter that he was there to bring them some local Guyanese money. I concluded they must have made a similar arrangement as Bunny Friemann did with his friend to receive Guyanese dollars. As soon as their uncle arrived Bonnie hurried over to him and her sister Dohne followed. Their uncle was an imposing, six foot four figure, well built with a full head of hair. Bonnie greeted him with a big hug and then rested her head gently on his chest, her hands around his midsection. She embraced him for so long that Dohne had to stand there waiting to get a hug. They ended up with him holding one on each arm. They were both holding on to their uncle so tenderly and with such obvious affection that their brother Brian ran over and insisted they pose for pictures. It was a very touching scene. Holding his nieces around their waists, he walked with them to our table and was introduced. After chatting for a few minutes with us, he turned and made his way to the parking lot still clutching his nieces as he departed.

At the breakfast table the conversation turned to what we each were going to do for the day. We had all agreed to attend the benefit party at the Fernandes compound, so that was set.

A few of us indicated we would go to the Georgetown Club to speak to the student we helped sponsor at the University of Guyana. Peter Headecker said Bonnie was thinking of getting in a few rounds of golf. "She likes the game and she's good," he said with a certain pride, a smile coming to his face as he spoke. "What do you mean 'she is good'?" asked Bunny Friemann. "So you play together?" asked someone else before he could answer.

"We played together occasionally from time to time but she is more passionate about it." Then he went to explain. "One time I went out to play with her and at the end of nine holes I was two strokes ahead. Boy, I thought I had her!" he said with a wide smile. "Suddenly she turned to me and asked, 'What is the score?' When she realized she was behind she began bearing down. By the time the game ended she was ahead by one stroke. She's very competitive," he said smiling broadly. It was clear he knew how to be in charge without taking charge, as I saw when he interacted with his family.

I left to go into Georgetown, to walk around on my own before going to our meeting. In setting off for the city I thought I would try something. I told the clerk at the desk I wanted a taxi to go into town but I could pay only $1000 for the trip. He said that simply could not be done, because the rate was $1500. We argued for a few seconds when I told him I would find a taxi on the public road. He informed me that taxis and minibuses rarely stopped outside the hotel, and yet a minibus did for me after a few minutes. As I got on I noticed there were two vacant seats, the one I was about to take, and another. Within half a mile we picked up someone else. The minibus deposited me in the centre of town, the fee to my surprise was $100 Guyanese. The cost of public transportation was indeed reasonable. I arrived at the Georgetown Club for our meeting with John Carpenter and the student we sponsored at the University of Guyana.

Upon my arrival, the guard emerged from his post and let me in. The first thing that struck me was the place was as quiet as a church. There was literally no one around. As I walked in, I passed by a number of tropical flowers and a golden apple tree laden with fruit. Rather than go in, I took a quick look in the rear where there was a second building at the edge of the property lined with fruit trees and interspersed with flowers. The downstairs area, which I had seen a few days earlier at dawn, had a wide portico that extended with a wooden dais for a band. The croquet court where people played all dressed in white years ago no longer retained the smooth surface it once had. Upstairs, the place was just as empty, except for Romeo Pereira sitting in front of a table as John Carpenter arranged his files. The club upstairs remained as the British had left it. A simple ballroom-like expanse with a rather small bar tucked in one corner. Everything about its architecture smacked of the era in which it was built. The wide polished floor was slightly uneven in sections partly brought on by age, and the putty between the planks was missing in a few places. One could see the place was well maintained, but it looked worn. The estate windows facing the street gave the space a colonial feel. The place was no longer a hive of activity. Gone were all the British expatriate managers, all of the company executives, their wives and children who kept the place humming with activity from morning to night, especially on a Saturday. Almost in an instant they had all vanished, as though blown away by a fierce wind.

Carpy greeted me and handed me a file that covered the academic life of the student we had sponsored. Shortly after I arrived Cyril Da Silva and a number of others turned up. I was surprised to see Bobby Fernandes there already. The young student, Kezia Abika Bess, arrived five minutes late so that gave us time to go through her resume among ourselves beforehand. Her transcript was superb. She was an excellent student while at

St. Stanislaus and so far had excelled at the University of Guyana as well. She planned to major in chemistry and minor in biology and was good at athletics to boot. Once I had a chance to peruse her transcripts I could see why John Carpenter had taken such an interest in her. When Kezia arrived, I was surprised to see a painfully shy wisp of a young woman, about five feet tall and no more than one hundred pounds. Carpy had her sit next to him, sensing she would be nervous. She sat with her shoulders leaning forward and her eyes focused on the papers and files on the table where the story of her life and future was reduced to four pages, and two pages of her agreement with us. Carpy gave her a nice introduction and then invited questions. A few people asked questions which she answered haltingly at first. When someone chimed in to say that this was not an interview but instead a reinforcement of our commitment to her, she seemed to relax a little. Sensing how shy and awkward Kezia Bess was in our presence Carpy announced he would invite her and her mother to the benefit we were all attending that evening as his guest. Most of my friends took Carpy's gesture in stride, realizing how much it would mean to a person of humble background like Kezia's. Our meeting with her lasted less than an hour.

After the meeting was finished, I took the opportunity to look around the room more closely. I was examining the faded photographs on the wall when Carpy joined me. He took me around to each of the photographs and, like a tour guide, gave me a little talk explaining each of them. Most were pictures of Georgetown years before, and of a few stalwarts of the club. He explained there were eleven rooms upstairs and two additional rooms in the rear all for guests. The club was not the sumptuous place I thought it would be but, by today's standards, I found it quaint.

With the meeting over so quickly I thought I might go to visit Mrs. Fraser in Lamaha Gardens. Until his death a few months earlier, her husband had been the agent for my family's property all these years, and I had always made time to visit them in Brooklyn every summer when they came for holiday. She welcomed me warmly and expressed her joy at seeing me on this side of the Caribbean. Her house was built on an area that Dale Morgan and I frequented when it was just a field slated for the construction of senior government personnel housing.

After a pleasant visit, I walked down the road admiring the many stately homes in the area. I walked past Bel Air Road which used to be called Milky Bank Trench, a name given the area when sugar cane laden punts stirred up the water as they passed along years before. I stopped at a few small shops along the way for chat with patrons. Once I reached Sheriff Street I summoned a taxi for my hotel.

The party that evening was a long standing annual event to benefit the St. Joseph Mercy Hospital held at the Fernandes compound. Most of us had been there before as students to visit our classmates, Bobby and Billy, or to other events held there. The Fernandes family had, from the inception of its success in business, engaged in philanthropy in one way or another especially towards the Catholic church and Catholic organizations.

The benefit was not particularly well attended that evening but those who did come seemed to be enjoying themselves. Dale Morgan sat at a table for most of the evening while his son Colin remained close by. He looked tired but claimed he was not. He said he had resolved many pending personal problems, and felt that being away from home had helped him to do so. Colin, always with a ready smile on his face, was still enjoying his Guyana experience as he and his father were due to depart the following day.

For me the highlight of the party was seeing both Bobby and Billy Fernandes dancing with their wives, showing no signs of their illness as they worked their way around the floor, each in a tight embrace.

I was sitting with my back to our table looking at couples on the dance floor. I must have become lost in a fog because when I turned around I found that I was suddenly alone. I looked around the crowd to see where everyone went and saw Dale Morgan and Colin at the other end of the compound chatting with Bonnie and Peter Headecker in a group. Bunny Friemann was off at John Carpenter's table chatting with Colleen who had a large party of guests at their table. I must have been so far away in thought that I did not see or hear them depart from our table. As I breathed in the heavy scent of the gardens surrounding the property I was overtaken by a gloomy train of thought. I began to think of the city I had lost. The country I no longer belonged to. I thought of my cousins in Trinidad, some of whom I had just visited and my cousins in Ellerton, St. George Barbados with whom I had completely lost touch. I was still lost in my private thoughts gaping at the dance floor when my attention was attracted by two young women who appeared suddenly and took the seats at a table next to mine. From the corner of my eye I could see that they were swaying to the music and giggling while watching the dance floor. As the song finished, I saw them run over and hug Billy Fernandes and his wife who were one table over from theirs. By the time they returned to their seats I was thinking it was too bad my legs and feet hurt so much, as I would dearly have liked to ask one of them to dance. I was still debating with myself when I heard someone I was not aware of at my table say, "Burrowes, why don't you get up and dance with the girls?" I turned around and to my surprise it was Randy Bradford sitting with a woman next to him. His presence and request brought on a paralysis I could not explain. I said nothing in response. All I did was turn in his direction, smile slightly, and then return to gazing at the dance floor lost again in my own world. "Can't you see the girls want to dance. It's my daughter and her cousin. You have my permission," he said encouraging me. My response was to keep staring at the dance floor without explanation. I felt literally exhausted sitting there, still seeking and longing for something, and still embarrassing myself in front of my schoolmates.

TOUCH DOWN

I was sitting in the rear at an empty table having coffee with Bunny Friemann when Bonnnie and Peter came puffing into the dining room. They were both dressed in exercise clothes. "We went for a walk along the sea wall," Bonnie announced, still a little breathless. She went over to the coffee station as Peter sat down to relate their experience. They had both enjoyed their early morning walk along the sea-wall next to the Atlantic Ocean, passing in front of the many houses built to capture the breeze coming off of the water. Peter marvelled at the size of the houses, particularly that of the former President which was still under construction. "Where do these people get the money to build these fantastic places?" he asked in apparent bewilderment. "That house is at least ten thousand square feet!" Peter went on to express his surprise at seeing builders working that early on a Sunday morning so he went over and spoke to the guys pouring cement. As a building engineer and site manager in Canada, he was impressed at the quality of cement they were using and their skill at handling it. An easy smile broke over his face as he spoke of their expertise. It was a smile of pride acknowledging that these builders, his countrymen, had risen to a level far above what he imagined they could. When Bonnie returned to the table she joined in with her impressions of their walk announcing, "I could live here. It's growing on me. But there is no way I would drive on these roads." Listening to her utter those words seemed like a stunning turnaround from someone who was so ambivalent initially. As a matter of fact, just one week after we arrived the place no longer felt like a foreign country to many of us. While no one really contemplated rushing back to Guyana to take up permanent residence, the appearance of a transformed city and the energy of its citizens had grown on many of us. As Bunny Friemann put it, "The place is in my soul even as my heart is where my family is."

Shortly after 9:00 am my friend Cynthia arrived to take me to brunch. Cynthia, who had visited New York annually for the last three decades, has been my main physical link to Guyana. I would take her out to lunch or dinner and she would bring me up to date about friends, politics and changes taking place. When David Granger began publishing his new monthly magazine on culture and politics Cynthia got me a subscription. For the last decade she lamented the fact that I had not visited for so long. "I want to see what you think of the place," she would say. After speaking on the telephone several times and visiting her in her office at work, she pretty much was following the evolution of my views and feelings.

We went to the Herdmandson and its dining room was nearly full when we arrived. After speaking to the owners whom she knew, Cynthia got us seats even though we did not have reservations. She was really glad I was enjoying myself and re-connecting with Guyana, but was a bit puzzled that I adjusted so easily to the radical changes in the architectural landscape and the garbage strewn around. One of my main criticisms was not so much that the new constructions were too big but they were garish. The trouble was the houses we grew up in were much too small for today's lifestyle. They were built for a simpler time when Guyana emerged from an agriculture-based culture to a more urban one. Anyone who has been in the US and around the world knows of the aggressive growth that has taken place in most areas in the past two decades. They are also aware that phrases have been coined to disparage some of the changes, the "McMansion" for example, in sedate suburban areas. What is going on in Georgetown is part of an ongoing social development and change that is worldwide in its embrace. When we speak about the over-the-top style of architecture we are talking about taste, and that is a personal preference. Others prefer an architecture that reflects a more classic sensibility whereas many nouveau-riche businessmen want to show they are moving up or have arrived.

As for the garbage all around, I reminded my friend of what New York or Washington DC or London, where she once studied, looked like when we were students in the late 60's or early 70's. Garbage and decay were everywhere. Today, however, with public education and municipal awareness this has been reversed. On that basis I was hopeful, even as I was disappointed that things had fallen so far. Her latest source of irritation was the rapid disappearance of the bungalows for which the city was so famous. She thought the government should do something, perhaps have them declared a heritage site. But I pointed out that such a decision was a public one and not one usually made by government. It is only when people band together and make their voices heard by organizing others that governments take notice and respond.

Back at the hotel after my long brunch with Cynthia, I settled in to have drinks with my friends. Mark McWatt had departed but the rest of us were all awaiting our trip to Essequibo with anticipation. I left a little while later for a "lime", as he called it, with Horace and his drinking buddies a short distance away, opposite the Caricom (Commonwealth Caribbean Secretariat) headquarters. When I arrived at the "event" in a vacant lot, things had already started. Half of a pig was already on the personally designed BBQ and the people gathered there all had a drink in hand. Horace introduced me to his friends: Cecil Regiana with whom he worked as an international civil servant in Africa, the manager of the St.

Stanislaus Agriculture Farm a short distance away, and a few other people who worked as day labourers joined us. This was a regular gathering of a varied group of friends who came together to talk, to eat, and to have a drink. I had a spirited discussion with the well-known political operative and TV commentator, Ramon Gaskin. A former member of the PPP, now the governing party, he accused them all of betraying their philosophy of social justice in favour of personal greed. I gathered he felt the party had cast aside its true believers in favour of a technocratic elite whose main purpose was not to serve the people as he put it, but to serve themselves.

The four story office building next to which we were camped was owned by Cecil Rejana. He had constructed the building on that side of the road and in that place in anticipation that the edifice built to house the Caricom offices would run out of space and eventually turn to him. As it turned out that did not take very long to happen. When Caricom eventually did rent it from Cecil, Caricom's senior officers promptly followed suit because of the panoramic view of the East Coast Highway in the foreground and the wide Atlantic in the distance. It made for a picturesque and calming view for its occupants. "I benefit from their lack of foresight," Cecil Rojana claimed modestly as he showed me around the offices and the rooftop.

Rather than abating as it had often done in days past, the humidity seemed to increase as the day went along. This made my attempt to walk at least part of the distance back quite difficult. Dusk was falling quickly and, by the time I realized I needed a taxi none was around. It took some time but eventually I got one.

When I arrived at the hotel, I could see as I entered the dining room that Peter and Bonnie Headecker were entertaining a group of about twenty people who, I guessed, were Bonnie's uncle and his family. I wanted to join them and listen in on the conversation but better judgment prevailed. I did not allow them to see me as I slipped up to my room to watch the NCAA competition in the US where Connecticut women were playing Notre Dame in the semi-finals, and to read the local newspapers piling up on my desk.

Among the articles that caught my eye while perusing the newspapers were two by members of the Working People's Alliance (WPA) political party. The organization had started off as a vibrant alternative to the two established parties before my departure, but had failed to make the impact its leaders had hoped. From their complaints I concluded the party had not, in the time of my absence, moved beyond that of a debating society still railing against Forbes Burnham, a politician dead for nearly two decades. While he was alive they had accused him of corruption and of running an incompetent government based on the cult of personality. As members of the leading edge of large numbers of students studying abroad, they seemed to feel they should be in charge. When their titular leader, Walter Rodney, was killed in an unfortunate accident they accused President Burnham of having a direct hand in it. When investigation after investigation concluded that neither President Burnham nor his people was involved they refused to accept the findings. Instead they raised Walter Rodney to the status of patron saint as a tactic to win support. Among supporters, circumstances surrounding Walter Rodney's death gained the status of "conspiracy theory" like those in the US who believed the CIA killed JFK. All the while they opposed every project Forbes Burnham and his People's National Congress (PNC) party proposed, and they worked diligently to deflect his efforts to get international agencies like the World Bank to sponsor his pet hydro-electric program which would have clearly benefited the country today. Clearly they saw Forbes Burnham, the PNC, and the generation of 1953 as their impediment to office. After carping for a decade about rigged elections by the PNC, the group faced the electorate in internationally supervised elections. It turned out that, as a group, they lacked the mettle to go through the laborious and, at times, vexing and humiliating processes necessary to win an election. They seldom travelled beyond urban centres and they lost. Two decades after Burnham's and the PNC's departure, they now accuse the PPP government of the same sins. But their past accusations have returned to haunt them because many people see the PNC as being far more competent than the PPP. They question where the money is that they accused Burnham of stealing knowing that Burnham's wife died in near destitution and his children live very ordinary lives. Their main proposal now, as in the past, is that the winning party should form a national government; one, of course, that includes them. It is a sad end to an ambitious group of bright men and women who once basked in the privileges given them by a newly independent country, and whose jejune view collided with political reality, much to their dismay.

Against all odds the Connecticut women won the game against Notre Dame.

ESSEQUIBO

The last time I took a trip to the Essequibo, I had to take a ferry across the Demerara River, board a train to Parika then take a slow boat to the Essequibo Coast. It was a trip I had made many times from the age of seven. So it was with great eagerness that I looked forward to seeing the changes as we departed by bus at 6 in the morning for the Pomeroon. As I had come to expect by then everyone was punctual, even early. At that hour traffic was still light so we sailed up the East Bank Highway and crossed the Demerara Harbour Bridge at Providence. There we were joined by those who followed us to Parika in their SUVs. The road from Vreed-en-Hoop, now totally paved as a modern highway, allowed us to travel at a quick pace. As I peered through the windows I recognized nothing along the way. Even the sugar estates which came up to the roadside in some places were gone. Like Georgetown the houses had changed, many had become bigger and were built of concrete. When we passed the village of Leonora, someone in our party pointed out a barely functioning supermarket complex built next to the police station. He related that the owner built the complex thinking it would be safe at its location. What happened instead was that the police themselves continuously ran up large bills which they then refused to pay, so the market eventually had to close.

Once we reached Parika I recognized the old stelling immediately. The village itself had matured into a small town with well-defined streets. The fruit and vegetable stands were full. Rather than go onto the stelling to catch our boat, the bus turned and wound its way down a narrow road. We passed three sawmills and a number of modest houses along the way. What piqued my interest, however, was the number of landings at which several boats were moored. All of the boats had a different profile than I remembered, and they all had very powerful engines. I could not understand why all of the boats down to the last one had undergone such a drastic change in design. There were also several high speed transport vessels and I wondered why. Did the population increase that much? Or did people travel more now that there was transportation readily available? The bus stopped at the landing owned by the uncle of Cyril Da Silva. He was a man in his early eighties, slim, agile and alert. He moved like a man half his age, and was as sharp as a tack. He had been a captain on the Essequibo and other rivers in the old days when the only means of transport were the slow steamers run by the then Transport and Harbours Department. We boarded two of his high speed transports and, after the crew was satisfied that we put on our life vests and fastened them properly, we departed. As we left the landing rain began to fall, first a drizzle, then a torrential downpour. It was high tide when we left and the water on the river was milky in colour. The strong wind made our ride bumpy and uncomfortable, especially for those of us who had taken up places in the rear, open to the elements.

As our destination at Supenaam came into view I was eager to see the place where I had spent so much of my youth. At the north of the river I recognized the AH Mazarally and Sons sawmill lying idle but as we passed it to get to the stelling to disembark, I recognized nothing else. It was chilling. I looked around frantically for my old house which used to be the first house on the road leading from Supenaam to Charity, the town where the road ended, but I could not recognize it. Both Supenaam and Charity always had a certain importance not only because of geographic locations, but because that was where government compounds for civil servant housing and offices were located.

Then I saw the house standing there, still intact, faded and abandoned. I was shocked. I stood there in the crowd waiting for our transport, speechless. The stelling was crowded with boats waiting to depart and with a few just arriving. All were supped-up boats similar to those seen on the rivers in Southeast Asia. If I were living in Guyana I would have looked around and thought it was magical, but as a visitor I was a little sad. Because it was still drizzling, I did not stray from the group or attempt to locate anything or speak to anyone. I took in everything from where I stood.

My family and I had arrived in Supernaam nearly sixty years ago to the day. I was seven years old and my father, Reynold Burrowes, was transferred from New Amsterdam to assume the post of Government Dispenser, essentially a pharmacist, charged with responsibility for a particular area. It was a big promotion. We arrived in Supernaam after a day of travel. We departed Georgetown at 8:00 am, took the train from Vreed-en-Hoop to Parika and then the "steamer" to Adventure. On the steamer we travelled first class so we had one of the three cabins available for the four hour trip. The steamer, the *MV Poris* built in Glasgow, Scotland was slow and had a deep draft so sailors had to be constantly on the lookout for sand bars to avoid getting stuck. We arrived at Adventure around 3:00 pm and got into the only hired car on the Essequibo Coast, at that time a black Humber Hawk. We travelled down the red dirt road with a cloud of dust trailing us as we drove in quick succession past desolate villages with giant expanses of rice fields around them. When we arrived at Supernaam my mother burst into tears upon seeing our new home. It looked like an odd dwelling from its construction. It was dilapidated, standing some fifteen feet in the air on stilts and was in a state of total disrepair. We all sat in the car for some twenty seconds before my father opened the door and we children followed him. As we made our way up the steps we discovered one stair loose because of dry rot so we had to skip past it. It was only after we went in and looked around and returned to the car that my mother went inside. Supernaam was a remote place and every aspect of life was basic or primitive. Having had her cry my mother adjusted quickly to the slower tempo of life in the bush. The only people who came down the road that did not belong to the village came to see my father, the Government Dispenser. Most arrived by walking or occasionally by hired car. No more than a half a dozen vehicles travelled on the red dirt road, and my brothers and I were in the habit of betting whose vehicle was approaching from the beat of the engine and the plume of dust it kicked up as the dry season approached. In the wet season cars got stuck in the mud and, further up the coast, buses got stuck. Dr. Whaling, who drove down every Saturday stopping at any white flag on a stick to see a sick patient, would send word to say he was not coming because of the roads.

As I prepared to depart from Supenaam to Charity, I was looking at a modern road filled with minibuses and people milling around trying in the early morning to get to their destinations. I was looking at the realization of a dream many people had long ago. It was strange but it was good. I was transfixed by the sight that I missed getting into a minibus with Bunny Friemann, and yet another with Peter and Bonnie Headecker. I finally rallied and caught the last bus with Mrs. Carpenter, Paula Vieira, a few other wives, and other guests who joined us for the day. We took off so quickly that I did not have time to take in the new developments we passed. It was like travelling on the high speed trains of Europe. Before I knew it we were three miles away at Aurora. All the while I was saying aloud thoughtlessly, "I don't see the Sahoy Estate," or "Where is Adventure?" I became aware my muttering might be disturbing Paula Vieira. Sitting next to her sister in her sun glasses she whispered something that alerted me. But when I passed Suddie, the administrative centre for the country and the government compound I began to question aloud once again, "Where is the Catholic Church? I don't see the Catholic Church." "Oh, he is looking for places," she said to her sister. After that she did not seem to mind my babbling to myself. Eventually the conductor came to my rescue and began to point out different landmarks as we went by.

We stopped at the Bacchus Shopping Complex at Affiance for breakfast. Always a more popular village, Affiance had been home to the owners of the bus franchises that serviced the dirt roads along the Coast. Once off the bus, we all crowded into the small café to enjoy a breakfast that had already been prepared. Among the offerings I saw on display were slices of pizza. Boy was I surprised! I realized then how deeply modern culture had penetrated a place I thought would still be backward. The surprise was on me. When I spoke to some of the workers they informed me the whole of the Essequibo had been electrified. They had their own backup generators if needed, and they hastened to add that they seldom did. One person said with confidence, "We have everything here. We even have an MRI machine at Suddie hospital." All I could do was smile at his remark. The people I spoke to had no idea that just a short while ago their village was one of the most distant and backward places in the Caribbean. They didn't know and it was obvious to me they did not care. It was good to see. Their confidence in the future is probably the reason why so many of the taxis whizzing by on the roads flew the national flag.

The last of the sugar estates that once lined the Essequibo Coast was abandoned by Bookers in the 1920's. Since then people had done rice farming. With rice in greater demand

and prices better and more consistent, the farmers were doing well. When we reached Charity I had the same experience as I did at Supenaam. Total bewilderment. Three story buildings dominated the landscape. After orienting myself I recognized the hospital and medical compound, but that was all. The daily market was in full tilt, teeming with vendors selling an abundance of fruit and vegetables. I took a quick walk through the market and then ran over to get into the boat about to take off for John Carpenter's farm. It was a smaller boat and carried just a few people. It rode low in the water, but its powerful engine pushed it along quickly. With the sun in my face I put my hand in the water and allowed it to skip through my open fingers as we went. It was nice being on the river once again even for a short ride. It all felt very satisfying.

As I was on the first boat to arrive at the farm, I took the opportunity to look around on my own. I ran into the farm manager, Vladimir Calderia. He told me the farm belonged to his family before it was sold to John Carpenter and Gerry Gouveia. In one barn was the equipment for drying coffee. In another I found a giant Lister generator. The size of the engine and the distinctive sound it made distinguished it as one from an era long past.

Upon returning to the house, I ran into a classmate who was joining us for the first time William Campbell. "I know you, you won that elocution competition," was the way he greeted me. I flashed a smile. I recognized him also. That he should remember the only highlight of my undistinguished high school life these many years later was a surprise. I remembered how dejected I was at how poorly attended the final competition was. Then I remembered that he was a finalist also. Both he and I were Essequibo boys who were going to school in Georgetown, he from the Cameroon and we were always friendly towards each other. Like he did me, Bunny Freimann had prevailed upon him to travel home so as to attend even a single event with us.

Once the others arrived we gathered in an area on the ground floor clearly set up for long days of relaxation. The fruits came out and the bar was opened. Some took chairs and settled in for a pleasant time. Others, myself among them, went for a nature walk with John Carpenter as our guide. Mrs. Carpenter promptly headed to the house to make sure the kitchen staff was on time and on course. She had accompanied her husband John to every event we attended. A slim woman of medium height and athletic in her movements, she was charming to us men and tried to make sure the women enjoyed the outing even though it was an occasion for the boys. She handled her role with aplomb and was a back-up to her husband who consulted her openly on several occasions.

During our walk with John, I pointed out to Bunny Friemann that the farms around did not seem to cultivate any new crops in the past decades. The coffee, orange and avocado trees were all in different stages of bloom. The back of the property ended where the pegasse began. The front of the property was planted with different tropical flowers, a variety of local orchids and, to my astonishment, Carpy knew the name of every one of the flowers on his property. He was very proud of the golden shower orchids in bloom at the time. Halfway around the perimeter of the farm, rain began to fall and some chose to return to the house while others of us continued on. When we returned, those who had remained behind were attacking the assortment of food that had been prepared. It was a wonderful feast put on by Mrs. Carpenter. So wonderful that Peter Headecker fell asleep afterwards which prompted Carpy to joke, "Long ago we used to say he is suffering from niggeritis. Now to be politically correct, we say he is suffering from ethnic fatigue."

Several of us began questioning John Carpenter about the reason for the changes we had seen. He explained that the transportation system along the Essequibo developed as a reaction to the policy of the Burnham government. The inability to import many items because of the government embargo presented the country with its "prohibition moment". Businessmen took a limping transportation system started by merchants along the coast and upgraded it to import banned items from Venezuela or Trinidad. That was why high speed boats became fashionable. The boats were designed to carry heavy loads at a high speed through shallow rivers. What made the whole thing curious was that the bridge across the Demerara River had just been erected by the government, but it turned out to be crucial in moving volume into the city of Georgetown and beyond. Soon after the price of gold began to skyrocket. Gold, which diamond miners had routinely dismissed, became quite valuable and once again high speed boats were pressed into service as many people made their way to those areas in search of fortune.

After spending about five hours at Carpy's place on the Pomeroon River he corralled us all and we departed. Carpy himself was insistent from the time the trip was announced that he absolutely did not want to be on the river at night. Once we got onto the minibuses for our return to Supenaam, they took off. We arrived first so I took the time to speak to a few people milling around. One person pointed me to the son of my neighbour and childhood friend, Oscar Stephens. We chatted for a few minutes until the other buses arrived. Soon after getting on the boats for Parika a light rain began to fall once again. As we went along the light rain gave way to fog and darkness descended much earlier than usual. Travelling in a high speed boat through rain and fog was clearly a concern to the driver, as he got on his walkie-talkie to notify the people at the landing of his position on the river. He lowered his speed when the waves began to buffet the boat. As we rounded the turn heading for home port the driver called ahead to say he could not see the stelling. Though I was concerned sitting next to him, I enjoyed feeling what it must have been like running contraband back in those days. After constant chatter between the driver and home base, they informed him they had put the spotlights on for him. Still he could not see them. "You have to blink the lights," he urged. It was only then he knew where the landing was. Though we were never in any real danger I could tell everyone was worried. As if by miracle the rain stopped just we began to disembark. The ride back was a silent one as we passed villages with lights and people actively going about their business in the evening.

TYING UP

I said goodbye to Peter and Bonnie and their party at breakfast. They were all due to depart later in the day and I was taking off to wrap up a few things on my last full day in Guyana. I took a taxi to the Kingston offices of A.H. Mazaharally and Sons to see my old friend Yacoob Mazaharally. Our families had become friends in the mid 1950's when, a year or two after we moved to Supenaam Essequibo his father, after making good money as a rice farmer, purchased the sawmill and moved his family from the Corentyne to Supenaam. Our families became even better friends when my father discovered that their eldest daughter, Dolly, was married to his high school friend George Bulkhan.

I was greeted by Yacoob's assistant and led into his office where he sat in a high-back executive chair. After rising to greet me Yacoob sat me opposite him. His first words to me were, "Why did you take so long to come and visit me?" For a moment I was surprised, but I quickly replied, "I wanted to go to Supenaam first and to look around Georgetown." He seemed genuinely disappointed he was not among the first people on my list to visit. He knew of my impending arrival from a note in the Stabroek News and he had practically ordered my brother, his employee, to ensure I would pay him a visit. After giving some lame excuse I began to ask about his siblings. As with most Guyanese families his siblings had scattered. I enquired about Gloria in Pakistan and May-May in Brazil, about Shina and Halima who died in Canada, and

I remembered his brothers Mozam, Azam and Junior all of whom had died in Guyana. Even though they were his siblings Yacoob was a generation away in age from the older children. He was the last child, and was fifteen years younger than the oldest. That made him the second generation to run his family's business. From behind his desk I could see he had aged gracefully. He had the same face even though he had put more weight on a once slender frame. I could see from his speech that he was still a man of energy, just as he was growing up as a lad. When I told him my friend John Carpenter had told me about his swank birthday celebration a few days earlier, he again chastised me for not making contact, thereby explaining my not being invited. He said he wanted also to take me to Rupununi to visit his farm which is managed by his son. I gathered from the way he spoke that he was proud of the boy and especially of the job he was doing on his own. When I learned he had his own plane and would have flown me there, I realized I had made an unfortunate mistake in not visiting him earlier. We chatted for some time about the Essequibo, politics in the US and about our families. When I was on my way out of his office I saw a picture on the wall of the "old man", as we all called his father behind his back. I turned to him and said, "You look quite a bit like your old man." He did not quite agree.

Once I departed I thought seriously about visiting a few politicians who had expected me to call but I decided they would add no real substance to my visit so I caught a taxi for the General Post Office building to see my cousin Greta. She was dressed in a grey suit and sat behind a large desk with files carefully arranged on it. It was over forty years since we last met and while she had put on weight, the same genial personality came through immediately. She had the same quick smile and sparkling eyes and she spoke with the authority of someone accustomed to giving orders. We chatted about our families, from which I gathered she had taken on the role of matriarch.

She insisted she was absolutely not interested in politics but went on to give me a clear eyed analysis of the problems between the City Council and the central government. Her office itself was sparsely decorated with no photographs of her family or state officials, and the furniture was clearly dated. As she spoke, I could not help admiring how much she had matured. We lamented the fact that I did not get to meet her family, but we parted promising to do so next time.

By the time I left it was nearly midday. I decided I had enough so I rang my brother Arthur and arranged to meet for lunch. Before having lunch we made a quick visit to say goodbye to Aunt Olga. The last visit I had to make was an obligatory one. I grabbed a taxi and gave the driver the address of my Uncle Frank Collins, with whom I had to discuss a delicate family matter. Frank Collins was once married to my father's sister Vera, Aunt Olga's twin sister. Their marriage fell apart when Uncle Frank, a policeman at that time, was transferred to the interior and left Aunt Vera and their four children in the city. The relationship between him and his family remained rocky at best, but his oldest son, Frank Jr. sent him a small stipend from the US every month. When my cousin Frank, who never married, died suddenly, his property went to his father because he left no will. At that point Uncle Frank eagerly assumed the role of father, which he had long ago abandoned, and wanted his son's house sold and the money sent to him. This was despite the fact that Frank Jr.'s sister lived nearby and had been promised the house by her brother.

Even the taxi driver had great difficulty finding the address. It was an odd one I had never heard of, nor understood. The address was 1283 South Sofia B. Field. Approaching the address from the city as we did, we went from paved roads to roads with potholes, to an area that was clearly not part of the city. Upon arrival I could see the address was a sugar estate designation, and stood on the periphery of a recently defunct sugar estate.

The family next door left their yard and went into the house to let Uncle Frank know he had a visitor. Upon emerging from his bedroom, he looked frail as he walked towards me. At six foot two he never weighed more than one hundred and sixty pounds. Now he seemed to be thirty pounds lighter. While he was in good health at 91, he had lost much of his hearing in one ear, a fact he seemed to use to his advantage. After the usual reports of how his daughter and grandchildren in the US were doing, his hearing seemed to become problematic as we talked about the sale of the house. Once I laid all of the cards on the table I felt my job was done. He rose and escorted me to the door insisting he see me off. I got into the waiting taxi and headed for the hotel. I wanted to relax before preparing for my departure early next morning.

Looking back, no one is more surprised than I that I decided to make the United States my home after leaving school. Prior to that, I had worked diligently to study the history, geography and politics of my homeland. So entrenched was I in all things Guyanese and Caribbean that even the mere mention I might remain in the US after my education offended me.

Slowly, however, I found myself increasingly immersed in American culture. After my marriage and the birth of my son those roots became profoundly anchored by family ties.

Still, however, Guyana tugged at my heartstrings. Despite the many years of my departure, warm memories of my Guyanese family and friends flooded my senses and penetrated my soul. I longed to retrace those steps of long ago and reconnect with the homeland I left so abruptly. But as the years and the decades passed, as new memories crowded out the old, as new obligations took precedence in my life, that reconnect was put on hold.

When it did materialize some 40 years later, when I finally ventured back to recapture some of the magic of my happy and promising youth, I came to realize that the proverbial "ties that bind" had indeed been loosened. The intervening years spent abroad had rendered me a virtual stranger in my mother country. Yes, the friendships had endured and the family I left behind welcomed me heartily, but deep inside I felt an estrangement I would never before have thought possible. I thought constantly of my return home. Home to the US, home to my son and home to the life in my adopted country. Now I was finally able to say goodbye.